LEGITIMATING IDENTITIES
The Self-Presentations of Rulers and Subjects

Rulers of all kinds, from feudal monarchs to democratic presidents and prime ministers, justify themselves to themselves through a variety of rituals, rhetoric, and dramatisations, using everything from architecture and coinage to etiquette and portraiture. This kind of legitimation – self-legitimation – has been overlooked in an age which is concerned principally with how government can be justified in the eyes of its citizens. Rodney Barker argues that at least as much time is spent by rulers legitimating themselves in their own eyes, and cultivating their own sense of identity, as is spent in trying to convince ordinary subjects. Once this dimension of ruling is taken into account, a far fuller understanding can be gained of what rulers are doing when they rule. It can also open the way to a more complete grasp of what subjects are doing, both when they obey and when they rebel.

RODNEY BARKER is Reader in Government at the London School of Economics. His publications include *Political Ideas and Political Action* (editor, 2000), *Political Ideas in Modern Britain in and after the Twentieth Century* (1997), *Politics, Peoples, and Government: Themes in British Political Thought since the Nineteenth Century* (1994) and *Political Legitimacy and the State* (1990).

LEGITIMATING IDENTITIES

The Self-Presentations of Rulers and Subjects

RODNEY BARKER

CAMBRIDGE UNIVERSITY PRESS

PUBLISHED BY THE PRESS SYNDICATE OF THE UNIVERSITY OF CAMBRIDGE
The Pitt Building, Trumpington Street, Cambridge, United Kingdom

CAMBRIDGE UNIVERSITY PRESS
The Edinburgh Building, Cambridge CB2 2RU, UK
40 West 20th Street, New York, NY 10011-4211, USA
10 Stamford Road, Oakleigh, VIC 3166, Australia
Ruiz de Alarcón 13, 28014 Madrid, Spain
Dock House, The Waterfront, Cape Town 8001, South Africa

http://www.cambridge.org

First published 2001

Printed in the United Kingdom at the University Press, Cambridge

Typeface Baskerville Monotype 11/12.5 pt.   *System* LATEX 2$_\varepsilon$ [TB]

A catalogue record for this book is available from the British Library

Library of Congress cataloguing in publication data

ISBN 0 521 80822 7 hardback
ISBN 0 521 00425 X paperback

For
Helen

Contents

Acknowledgements   *page* viii

1 Legitimacy and legitimation   1

2 Legitimating identities   30

3 King John's Christmas cards: self-legitimation   41

4 Cousins at home and abroad   70

5 Rebels and vigilantes   89

6 Citizens   106

7 Conclusion   136

Bibliography   141
Index   158

Acknowledgements

I have drawn on 'Whose Legitimacy? Elites, Nationalism and Ethnicity in the United Kingdom', *New Community*, 21, 2 (April 1995),
and 'The Long Millennium, the Short Century, and the Persistence
of Legitimation', *Contemporary Politics*, 6, 1 (2000) for parts of this
book.

CHAPTER I

Legitimacy and legitimation

WHAT THIS BOOK IS NOT ABOUT

There is a convention sometimes found amongst academics of beginning books and articles with an inaugural lecture in reverse. Whereas the inaugural lecture conventionally opens with a series of polite tributes to predecessors, showing how the speaker is doing no more than standing on the shoulders of giants, making an inadequate attempt to fill the majestic shoes of exceptional predecessors, and simply acting as a feeble stand-in, the reverse can occur once the scholar is released from ceremonial restraints and unleashed on the wild world of monographs and journals. This reverse version lists all those who have in any way touched on the author's subject, and condemns them as theoretically impoverished, empirically threadbare, and intellectually sterile. Their crime usually turns out to have been the rather different one of failing to have contributed to the author's own enterprise because they were in fact doing something quite different. Historians of the poor law are dismissed for not having provided policy recommendations for twentieth or twenty-first-century governments, writers on political rhetoric for not having dealt with the distribution of capital, and analysts of trade unionism for having ignored conspiracies in the cabinet. So might the author of *Winnie the Pooh* be dismissed for having failed to contribute anything to the analysis of tactical voting.

I am not going to be so self-denying as to refuse from the outset to make any critical assessments whatsoever of any previous work. But my discussion of other authors will be designed to defend me against possible criticisms of the Winnie the Pooh kind, rather than

to make them. It may avoid misunderstanding if I say what I am
not doing, so that no one, or at least fewer people, will complain
that I have done it inadequately. This book is not about legitimacy.
Neither is it a criticism of those who have written about legitimacy –
I have written about it myself – although it argues that legitimacy
can frequently be a misleading term, applied beyond its proper and
useful scope. I begin by looking briefly at work which borders on
the topic of this book. My intention is not to dismiss an existing
body of work, but to mark off the boundaries, and the overlaps,
between that work and the subject of this enquiry. My intention
in the remaining chapters is to give a brief initial account of an
aspect of political life which deserves more attention, and whose
description can add to the richness of our overall picture. This book
is therefore an essay rather than a detailed historical or empirical
study, and relies on the work of others for its illustrative material.

The principal subject of the book is a characterising activity
of government, to which Max Weber has drawn attention in his
famous definition of the state as 'the human community which
(successfully) claims the monopoly of legitimate coercion'.[1] What
is not always noticed is that Weber is talking not about some abstract quality, 'legitimacy', but about an observable activity in which
governments characteristically engage, the making of claims. This
activity is mentioned by Weber as part of a definition of the state.
What characterises government, in other words, is not the possession of a quality defined as legitimacy, but the claiming, the activity
of legitimation. This book begins with the question, which is pro-
voked by Weber's definition: 'What are governments doing when
they spend time, resources and energy legitimating themselves?'
The question is one that is often hidden or obscured in the social
sciences, but is nonetheless more often present there than the
attention normally given to it suggests. When Anthony Downs
gave the apparently purely utilitarian account of government and
politics as involving the pursuit of income, prestige, and power,[2]

[1] Max Weber, 'Politics as a Vocation' in H. C. Gerth and C. Wright Mills (eds.), *From Max Weber: Essays in Sociology* (London, Routledge & Kegan Paul, 1948), p. 78.
[2] Anthony Downs, *An Economic Theory of Democracy* (New York, Harper & Brothers, 1957), p. 28: 'From the self-interest axiom springs our view of what motivates the political actions of party members. We assume that they act solely in order to attain the income, prestige, and power which come from being in office. Thus politicians in our model never seek

only the first member of the trilogy, income, was tangible, straight-forward, and relatively unproblematic: £100 is £100, and is twice as much as £50. Power is more complicated, since it is a metaphor for describing the fact that things happen, or do not happen. Does a government minister who introduces smaller class sizes, in so do-ing use, or enjoy, more 'power' than one who sponsors genetically modified maize? Does the same minister enjoy more power when she broadens the 'A' Level curriculum than when she assists music in primary schools. And is power an end in itself, or a means to acquire other things, or is it better understood as neither of these, but as a metaphor to describe success in acquiring them? But the complications of power are as nothing compared to those of pres-tige. Prestige is the least obviously utilitarian of them all, and seems almost to slip in hidden under the cloak of its rational companions in Downs's definition.

In giving the pursuit of prestige as one of the three aims of gov-ernment, Downs, far from being iconoclastic, is being thoroughly traditional. That other alleged exponent of a cynical pragmatic ap-proach to politics, Machiavelli, gave a remarkably similar account four centuries earlier, identifying the desire for prestige as one of the motives, and ends, of rulers.[3] Machiavelli speaks of greatness, hon-our, and prestige, whilst the material resources of government are little more than instruments for achieving these ends. Political sci-ence therefore gives plenty of precedent for paying attention to the seemingly non-utilitarian activities of rulers. And though the term 'prestige' can have a wide application, what is being described is a very particular kind of prestige, the prestige which applies to princes and presidents, kings and prime ministers, leaders and rulers. The claim of rulers to special status or qualities, and the actions they take in cultivating this claim, are the central part of endogenous legitimation, of the self-justification of rulers by the cultivation of an identity distinguished from that of ordinary men and women.

If the desire for prestige, for a sense of their unique identity, is a motive of rulers, how is such prestige to be identified, what

---

office as a means of carrying out particular policies; their only goal is to reap the rewards of holding office *per se*. They treat policies purely as a means to the attainment of their private ends, which they can reach only by being elected.'

3 Niccolò Machiavelli, *The Prince* ([1532] Cambridge, Cambridge University Press, 1988).

are its symptoms, how and where is it enjoyed, and by whom and under what conditions? What is the utility of such a seemingly non-utilitarian activity? It may be that the question cannot be answered, and that all that can be done is a preliminary clarification, not of an answer, but of the question. And it may be necessary to reject the question, and insist that a narrowly utilitarian account of politics is unhistorical and unempirical. Self-legitimation in the form of the cultivation of a distinguished identity may be a goal in itself. And to say that it is merely a means of justifying other goods is to leave unresolved the question of why such justification is desired or necessary in the first place. This desire or need for a very particular form of prestige was what Weber identified when he commented that 'in no instance does domination voluntarily limit itself to the appeal to material or affectual or ideal motives as a basis for its continuance. In addition every such system attempts to establish and to cultivate the belief in its legitimacy.'[4] When rulers legitimate themselves, they claim that particular species of prestige which attaches to government. Whether or not the apparently universal feature of government, the claiming of prestige, justification, authority, reflects a psychological need of government or of governors, lies outside the scope of this study or at least lies only at its very fringes. But the character and consequences of such endogenous or self-legitimation can still be studied with that question left to one side.

The intention in this book is to construct a preliminary sketch of a theory with as wide an historical application as possible. Two qualifications must be made. First, I have drawn for illustration on the evidence from both the United Kingdom and the rest of the world, and from a wide chronological range. This of itself means that there has been no intensive investigation or presentation of a particular instance of legitimation. The second qualification is that the conceptions of state, politics, and political identity and legitimation which I develop in the following pages are not directly addressed to what for many people has been the principal question associated with the terms 'legitimation' and 'legitimacy': are there criteria, both morally acceptable to the abstracted observer, and practically effective in the specific historical context, which operate

---

[4] Max Weber, *Economy and Society*, ed. Guenther Roth and Claus Wittich, 2 vols. (London, University of California Press, 1978), p. 213.

when regimes sustain their rule over a given population? But whilst not addressing that question, I suggest answers to other questions which will not be uncongenial to those who wish to do so.

THE CORONATION OF NAPOLEON

David's famous painting of the coronation of Napoleon and Josephine has two features of great interest for anyone looking at the way in which government is carried on, and the way in which rulers conduct themselves. The first feature is well known. Napoleon is himself placing the crown upon the head of the Empress Josephine. The significance of that is clear. The emperor is not ruling by the consent of anyone else: not the church, not God, and certainly not the people. He is exercising and expressing authority, his own authority. He is legitimate because he legitimates himself, and the coronation is in effect a self-coronation. This is not, in any obvious sense of the word, a democratic occasion. The second feature of the painting is less obvious. Not only is the immediate audience for this event relatively small and select, but the most important member of the audience is the emperor himself. The ritual is, above all, for his own benefit, telling him who he is, and how he is marked out from other men. The coronation serves to impress, not the emperor's subjects, but the emperor himself.

This inward-turning aspect of legitimation has until recently attracted relatively little attention. The principal interest of historians and political scientists has been in other features of the ritualistic actions of rulers. Most attention has been paid to legitimation as a means, not of convincing princes and presidents, but of convincing subjects. The self-legitimation of rulers was discussed by Weber, but has been partly obscured amongst other features of the legitimation of government, so that the complexity, and difficulties, of his account have largely been lost sight of. His account of self-legitimation slipped further and further into obscurity as attention was focussed on ways of describing politics and government which derived from other aspects of his work, or in reaction to what were criticised as its undemocratic, or anti-democratic, aspects. In a democratic century, which was at least the aspiration of the 1900s, rulers were seen as the beneficiaries of legitimation, rather than as either its focus or its centre. Not until the last two decades of the twentieth century did a renewed interest in the non-utilitarian side of government and politics lead to a slowly growing attention to the self-confirming, self-justificatory dimension of legitimation. The recognition of this element in Weber's theory has come, in particular, in formulating accounts of the collapse of communist regimes in Eastern Europe and the Soviet Union in 1989, though it can be found too in the work of social anthropologists such as Clifford Geertz.[5] What this recognition underlines is that such self-legitimation is not an un-usual or unique feature of one ruler of post-revolutionary France. In the world of everyday government, the language, etiquette, and rituals of self-legitimation are ubiquitous.[6] They are a feature of all government, and there is much to be gained from reminding ourselves of this, and giving a preliminary account and theory of legitimation at the centre, from the centre, and for the centre. When legitimation is seen from the centre outwards, rather than from the outside inwards, dimensions of government which have languished in the shadows are thrown into new, or renewed, relief.

THE RE-EMERGENCE OF GOVERNMENT

One of the features of the series of changes variously described as the end of the short twentieth century, the end of modernity, the end of the cold war, or the arrival of post-modernity, was a re-newed perception of government as an activity having its own pur-poses and ethos, one aspect of which was self-legitimation. When

---

[5] Clifford Geertz, *Negara: The Theatre State in Nineteenth Century Bali* (Princeton, Princeton University Press, 1980).

[6] Language is of course a problem. The terms used in languages other than English are often only roughly translated, and sometimes misrepresented, by the word 'legitimacy'. This qualification, whilst a very real one, is not unique to the study of legitimacy. In May 1992, during the popular demonstrations in major Thai cities which led to the restoration of a form of representative democratic government after a period of military intervention, the crowds were reported as shouting 'Down with the illegitimate regime!' Saitip Sukatipan, 'Thailand: The Evolution of Legitimacy' in Muthiah Alagappa, *Political Legitimacy in Southeast Asia: The Quest for Moral Authority* (Stanford, Stanford University Press, 1995), p. 218. Whatever they were shouting, it could not have been that. A similar problem can arise whenever the language of the system being studied is not English. Hok-lam Chan observes, in a study of legitimation in twelfth and thirteenth-century China, that 'legitimate succession' is an approximate translation only of the Chinese 'cheng-t'ung'. Hok-lam Chan, *Legitimation in Imperial China: Discussions under the Jurchen-Chin Dynasty (1115–1234)* (London, University of Washington Press, 1984), pp. 21–2.

the floodwaters of the short twentieth century (as Eric Hobsbawm has described the years from the Russian Revolution of 1917 to the collapse of East European and Soviet communism after 1989) retreated,[7] they revealed the hulks of government much as they had been when they were obscured by the waters of economic and social revolution eighty years before. The same priorities of rulers re-emerged, the same symbolic self-protection of government not only from outside doubts and the opinions of subjects and citizens, but from internal uncertainties of the kind that lead not to revolution but to abdication. If the great engagement of the twentieth century with the politics of class left behind the politics of place, religion, and nationality, it also obscured politics and government as self-generating activities, occupations with their own rewards, and their own justifications and legitimations. Not that these dimensions of government activity were absent during the short twentieth century nor that much sceptical writing was not eager to draw attention to them.[8] But ruling as a distinctive activity with its own aims, justifications, and culture was obscured by seeing government solely or principally as an instrumental activity. The three great standpoints of twentieth-century political science each sustained this vision. For Marxists, the state was either the instrument or the higher intelligence of capitalism; for democrats, it was the reflex or channel of popular or social pressures; for economic liberals it was, when behaving properly, the guardian of markets, and when behaving improperly the captive of socialists or the prisoner of socialist misconceptions. For none of them was it the institutional form of one of the major activities of humans and of human society, the exercise of power over the general affairs of other people.

EXISTING WORK

In the last twenty years of the twentieth century, political legitimation and political legitimacy attracted an increasing amount of

---

[7] Eric Hobsbawm, *Age of Extremes: The Short Twentieth Century: 1914–1991* (London, Michael Joseph, 1994).

[8] A variety of writers, from Michels and the early elitists to Orwell and the sceptical critics of power, from anarchists to post-Spencerian critics of bureaucracy, have identified the exercise of power as just as important as the objects for which it was ostensibly employed.

attention amongst political scientists, social scientists, and historians. This was in part in response to the end, and the circumstances surrounding and following the end, of the short twentieth
century: the replacement of communist regimes in Eastern Europe
and the Soviet Union by various forms of democracy; the emer-
gence, particularly with the development of the European Union,
of new forms of transnational governance; the conflicts between
democratic movements and party and military despotisms in Asia;
and the need to restate the conditions under which regimes legitimated themselves in a world where the simple polarities of com-
munist/capitalist, totalitarian/democratic, had either evaporated
or been intertissued with the dimensions of ethnicity, religion, and
national identity.

Within this growing body of literature on legitimacy and
legitimation,[9] there are three principal strands: normative assessment of legitimacy as a quality or possession of government;[10] the
study of popular attitudes towards and support for rulers as a basis
for analysing and predicting regime stability, both at national and
transnational level;[11] and the interweaving of the first two to form
a bridge or an alliance between is and ought.[12] Each strand is in

---

[9] The literature is extensive, and I have given samples only in the following footnotes.

[10] William Connolly (ed.), *Legitimacy and the State* (Oxford, Blackwell, 1984); Leslie Green,
The Authority of the State (Oxford, Clarendon Press, 1988); Tom R. Tyler, 'Justice, Self-
Interest, and the Legitimacy of Legal and Political Authority' in Jane J. Mansbridge,
Beyond Self-Interest (Chicago, University of Chicago Press, 1990), pp. 171–9.

[11] Muthiah Alagappa, *Political Legitimacy in Southeast Asia: The Quest for Moral Authority*
(Stanford, Stanford University Press, 1995); David Beetham and Christopher Lord,
Legitimacy and the European Union (London, Longman, 1998); Grainne de Búrca, 'The Quest
for Legitimacy in the European Union', *Modern Law Review* 59 (1996), 349–76; Soledad
Garcia (ed.), *European Identity and the Search for Legitimacy* (London, Pinter, 1993); James L.
Gibson and Gregory A. Caldeira, 'Changes in the Legitimacy of the European Court of
Justice: A Post-Maastricht Analysis', *British Journal of Political Science* 28, 1 (1998), 63–91;
Simon Hix, 'The Study of the European Union II: The "New Governance" Agenda and
its Rival', *Journal of European Public Policy* 5, 1 (1998), 38–65; Juliet Lodge, 'Transparency
and Democratic Legitimacy', *Journal of Common Market Studies* 32 (1994), 343–68; Heinz
Käufeler, *Modernization, Legitimacy and Social Movement: A Study of Socio-Cultural Dynamics and
Revolution in Iran and Ethiopia* (Zurich, Ethnologische Schriften Zürich, 1988).

[12] David Beetham, *The Legitimation of Power* (London, Macmillan, 1991); Jürgen Habermas,
Legitimation Crisis, trans. T. McCarthy (London, Heinemann, 1976); David Held, 'Power
and Legitimacy in Contemporary Britain' in Gregor McLennan, David Held and Stuart
Hall (eds.), *State and Society in Contemporary Britain: A Critical Introduction* (Cambridge, Polity,
1984); David Held, 'Crisis Tendencies, Legitimation and the State' in J. B. Thompson
and D. Held (eds.), *Habermas: Critical Debates* (London, Macmillan, 1982).

part an ideal type, and much work incorporates elements of more than one strand. But the three elements nonetheless give character to, and illustrate, the predominant approaches. The normative approach most frequently employs the terms 'legitimacy' and 'legitimate'. 'Legitimacy' is treated as a property or characteristic of regimes which satisfy criteria laid out by the observer. These criteria are most usually identified as the transfer of consent by subjects to rulers, often in some form of regularly renewed democratic contract. Procedural rules, respect for rights, the just exercise of governmental power, are frequently identified as supportive or additional criteria. Regimes which fulfil these criteria are then designated 'legitimate'. From within this tradition comes the argument for leaving the empirical or historical study of legitimation well alone, from those who argue that since there are ascertainable principles by which government can be justified, what is of principal importance is not the various claims that are made by rulers, or the various political rituals whereby support is expressed, but only the extent to which regimes approach acceptable norms of legitimacy. Normative political theory has been directed to developing a prescriptive theory of legitimacy, and has, in consequence, though not from logical necessity, been hostile to speaking of legitimacy in circumstances where the rulers, policies, or constitutions are considered morally unacceptable. The rulers are moreover perceived as agents rather than as actors, since the source of their legitimacy generally is presented as external to themselves. They are instruments of values whose origin lies elsewhere; the 'source of the legitimacy of the political process and the results it produces must lie ultimately outside the process'.[13]

The second, empirical or historical approach also rests most heavily on the terms 'legitimacy' and 'legitimate', which describe qualities of a political system, as opposed to 'legitimation' which describes an activity. Although the first approach is normative and the second empirical, the normative suppositions of the first are embedded in the second. The normative valuation of democracy guides research in the direction of studies of the opinions of voters

---

[13] Regina Austin, 'The Problem of Legitimacy in the Welfare State', *University of Pennsylvania Law Review* 130 (1982), 1510–18, p. 1514.

and of the efforts of government to influence these opinions. Legitimacy is used as a term to describe a regime which is supported by
its subjects,[14] and democracy is the most reliable manner in which
that support can be expressed and studied. Perceived in this way,
there is a phenomenon of legitimacy which can be numerically
measured.[15] Four different objections have been raised to this approach. The first is that the argument is circular, inferring consent
from obedience, and then invoking consent to explain obedience.[16]
Nothing, it is claimed, is added to an understanding of government
or politics by speaking of legitimacy in such a manner. The second
objection is that 'legitimacy' explains nothing, and is no more than a
redescription of the phenomenon being examined: support.[17] The
third objection, which leads on to the third manner of using the
terms, is that to describe as legitimate a regime which its subjects
believe to be legitimate is to empty the term of any moral content,
which content it ought to have.[18] A further, fourth objection can
be raised, which is that describing a resource of government, 'legitimacy', makes distinct or even optional an activity which is better
seen as integral to all government. If legitimacy is seen as a distinct
resource of government, it can equally be left out of account save

---

[14] David Easton, *A Systems Analysis of Political Life* (New York, John Wiley and Sons, 1965);
George Kolankiewicz, 'The Other Europe: Different Roads to Modernity in East-
ern and Central Europe' in Soledad Garcia (ed.), *European Identity and the Search for
Legitimacy* (London, Pinter, 1993); Juan J. Linz, *The Breakdown of Democratic Regimes: Crisis,
Breakdown, and Reequilibration* (Baltimore, Johns Hopkins University Press, 1978); John
Williams, *Legitimacy in International Relations and the Rise and Fall of Yugoslavia* (London,
Macmillan, 1998); David Beetham *The Legitimation of Power* (London, Macmillan, 1991);
Beetham and Lord, *Legitimacy and the European Union*; Frederick D. Weil, 'The Sources and
Structure of Legitimation in Western Democracies: A Consolidated Model Tested with
Time-Series Data in Six Countries Since World War II', *American Sociological Review* 54
(1989), 682–706.

[15] M. Stephen Weatherford, 'Measuring Political Legitimacy', *American Political Science Review*
86 (1992), 149–66.

[16] Rodney Barker, *Political Legitimacy and the State* (Oxford, Clarendon, 1990), pp. 56–60. Cf.
Joseph Bensman's comment that, in Weber's account, legitimacy cannot be dissected
out as a causal variable. Joseph Bensman, 'Max Weber's Concept of Legitimacy: An
Evaluation' in Arthur J. Vidich and Ronald Glassman (eds.), *Conflict and Control: Challenges
to Legitimacy of Modern Governments*, 17–48 (Beverley Hills, Sage, 1979).

[17] Brian Barry, *Sociologists, Economists, and Democracy* (London, Collier-Macmillan, 1970),
pp. 53–7.

[18] This argument is developed, for instance, by Peter G. Stillman, 'The Concept of Legitimacy', *Polity* (Amherst, North Eastern Political Science Association) 7, 1 (1974), 32–56,
p. 50; and David Campbell, 'Truth Claims and Value-Freedom in the Treatment of
Legitimacy: The Case of Weber', *Journal of Law and Society* 13, 2 (Summer 1986), 207–24,
p. 221, and by Beetham, *Legitimation of Power*.

in extreme situations, a deus ex machina to be called into account when all other explanations fail.[19]

The third manner of using the terms 'legitimacy', 'legitimate', and 'legitimation' involves constructing a theory with the aim of knitting together normative and empirical conceptions and theories.[20] It is in part a response to the phenomenon described by Rudyard Kipling, where

> the wildest dreams of Kew are the facts of Khatmandhu,
> And the crimes of Clapham chaste in Martaban.[21]

When this variety is confronted, the normative theory of legitimacy faces the problem that people have many different values, and that regimes which one observer regards as abhorrent nonetheless engage in justification, in legitimation, of themselves. One response of this position is to say that to treat legitimation in this manner is to confer approval on all kinds of distasteful regimes: on crooks, despots, and repressive incompetents. To go down this road is to lose any normative purchase on a concept which has value at its very core. The response to this is that an historical or empirical study of legitimation requires an acknowledgement of the variety of human political values. And whilst a democratic political science rests on strong normative and methodological grounds, much of government is not democratic, and normative aspirations should not prevent a study of a distinguishing feature of all government. The other response is to acknowledge that there are various modes of legitimation, but nonetheless to refine from each moral principles which can form a workable means of normative assessment.[22] But

[19] Even so sympathetic an analyst as Leslie Holmes, for instance, can write that 'communist leaderships typically attempt to move over time from predominantly coercion-based to predominantly legitimation-based power'. In the work of Margaret Levi legitimacy is given the role of an emergency generator, called into play only when other sources of explanatory power have failed. Leslie Holmes, *The End of Communist Power: Anti-Corruption Campaigns and Legitimation Crisis* (Cambridge, Polity, 1993) p. xiii; Margaret Levi, *Of Rule and Revenue* (London, University of California Press, 1988). This approach is to be found either stated or implied in a number of works, e.g. Rosemary H. T. O'Kane, 'Against Legitimacy', *Political Studies* 41, 3 (1993), 471–87. But see also Rodney Barker, 'Legitimacy: The Identity of the Accused', *Political Studies* 42, 1 (1994), 101–2.
[20] Beetham, *Legitimation of Power*; Habermas, *Legitimation Crisis*; Held, 'Power and Legitimacy'; Held, 'Crisis Tendencies'.
[21] Rudyard Kipling, 'In the Neolithic Age', quoted in Charles Carrington, *Rudyard Kipling: His Life and Work* (London, Macmillan, 1955; Harmondsworth, Penguin 1970), p. 195.
[22] Williams, *Legitimacy in International Relations*; Beetham, *Legitimation of Power*.

even if all and any regimes are considered, the question to ask will be, what point a regime has reached on whatever scale of progress or excellence the observer is employing, even if that scale is procedural rather than substantial. An objective measure of legitimacy is described which simultaneously takes account of the views or behaviour of the subjects of a government, and sets out criteria of its own, whereby, in a way that does not depend simply on the expression of opinion within the state studied, a regime can be judged either legitimate or not. Such an attempt to bridge the normative empirical divide acknowledges a variety of opinion, but insists on the participation of adult members of a community in the political process. This does not solve the problem, for a normative theorist, of a repressive regime actively supported by most of its subjects, but it does contribute towards a reconciliation of democratic theory with cultural difference.

These three bodies of social science constitute the bulk of recent and contemporary work on the topic. The principal contribution of existing work therefore has been either normative or centred on public opinion, on politics and democracy, rather than on government. But the new, or recovered, perspectives available with the end of the short twentieth century are not exhausted by these approaches.

The end of the cold war, post-modernity, the fading of the polarities of communism and anti-communism, have all cultivated a condition of things where legitimation within government, self-legitimation, has become far more evident. Governing is an activity legitimated in a myriad ways, and the absence of democratic legitimation will throw into relief how much legitimation is by government and *for* government. A post-modern, post-class world is likely to be one where the legitimating activities of government are cast into greater relief, once the justifying ends of government are more contested, and more varied.

NEW WORK

There is now a growing fourth body of work, which picks up on some underdeveloped, and subsequently largely neglected, elements in the work of Max Weber. This fourth body of work is the least developed, and the most dispersed, but it is expanding. It involves the study of legitimation as a self-referential or self-justifying activity characteristic of rulers, pursued with great intensity at the centre of government and with those engaged in the business of government as its principal consumers. This fourth body of work is an indication that government as a characteristic human activity is being given increased attention. For whilst legitimation may be conducted with reference to values external to government in a way which is congruent with the instrumental perspective on politics, it is conducted also with reference to the internal character of rulers, with claims to authority rather than to agency. It is worth returning briefly to Weber, because his arguments give a clue as to what is increasingly seen as a central feature of governing. Such a return has the additional benefit of allowing a correction of a well-established misunderstanding of what Weber was doing when he described legitimation. A neglected but central aspect of the work of Weber made a formative theoretical contribution by identifying the activity of legitimation, as distinct from the ascribed quality of legitimacy, as a defining characteristic of government, and one whose particular character and manner of expression varied with the formal and substantive character of the regime.[23] Weber's definition of the state as 'the human community which (successfully) claims the monopoly of legitimate coercion'[24] has been quoted frequently, and its significance as frequently not noticed. He was not arguing that governments needed some quality called 'legitimacy' to survive, nor that one of the things that governments sought was such a resource. His focus was upon an activity, legitimation or the making of claims to authority, which was one of the defining characteristics of all government. His principal depiction of it was as a constituting feature of government, and of its function within the apparatus of rule. The desire or even perhaps need for a very particular form of prestige was what Weber identified when he commented that 'in no instance does domination voluntarily limit itself to the appeal to material or affectual or ideal motives as a basis for its continuance. In addition every such system

[23] Weber, *Economy and Society*, Barker, *Political Legitimacy and the State*; C. Matheson, 'Weber and the Classification of Forms of Legitimacy', *British Journal of Sociology* 2 (1987), 199–215.
[24] Max Weber, 'Politics as a Vocation', in Gerth and Mills, *From Max Weber*, p. 78.

attempts to establish and to cultivate the belief in its legitimacy.'[25]
Weber is talking not about some abstract quality, 'legitimacy', but
about an observable activity in which governments characteristically engage, the making of claims.[26] What characterises government, in other words, is not the possession of legitimacy, but the activity of legitimation. Although this theory of legitimation has been
eclipsed by the normative and empirical discussion of legitimacy
as a property of some governments only, recent work has renewed
the examination of legitimation as a characteristic activity of all
government.

Going on from Weber's account, it is then possible to develop
a theory of legitimation which takes account of two neglected
components of government: legitimation as a characterising
activity of government, and the function of legitimation within
the governmental sphere and its relationship with the structure
and ethos of government. There is a growing body of work which
takes up this dimension of government, or which touches upon
it. Joseph Rothschild has argued that 'Discussions of legitimacy
and legitimation risk irrelevancy if they overlook this crucial dimension of the ruling elite's own sense of its legitimacy.'[27] Joseph
Bensman has commented that 'Legitimation as self-justification
is only validated inwardly'[28] and Jan Pakulski has identified
the self-legitimation of ruling elites as an important element in
Weber's argument and has applied this perception to the examination of Eastern Europe in general, and Poland in particular.[29]
David Beetham and Christopher Lord identify the need for legitimation in international government such as the European Union,
though they are reluctant to accept that it is significant within

[25] Weber, *Economy and Society*, p. 213.
[26] Joseph Bensman is particularly perceptive on the predominance of the claim, rather than its reception, in Weber's account. Bensman, 'Max Weber's Concept of Legitimacy'.
[27] J. Rothschild, 'Observations on Political Legitimacy in Contemporary Europe', *Political Science Quarterly* 92, 3 (1977), 42.
[28] Bensman, 'Max Weber's Concept of Legitimacy', p. 32.
[29] Jan Pakulski, 'Ideology and Political Domination: A Critical Re-appraisal', *International Journal of Comparative Sociology* 28, 3–4 (1987), 129–57; Jan Pakulski, 'Poland: Ideology, Legitimacy and Political Domination' in Nicholas Abercrombie, Stephen Hill, and Bryan S. Turner (eds.), *Dominant Ideologies* (London, Unwin Hyman, 1990); Jan Pakulski, 'East European Revolutions and "Legitimacy Crisis"' in Janina Frentzel-Zagórska (ed.), *From a One-Party State to Democracy*, 67–87 (Amsterdam, Rodopi, 1993).

states.[30] Empirical and historical work, for instance on medieval and seventeenth-century kingship,[31] on the art and architecture of government,[32] or on communist and post-communist regimes in Eastern Europe[33] has dealt with specific instances of this endogenous or self-legitimation. Self-legitimation was as important to Henry III, spending up to two years' entire royal revenue on creating Westminster Abbey as a justification of his own kingship,[34] as it was for the leaders of Eastern European regimes for whom a collapse of their own confidence in their authority was as important a factor in the fall of communism as were the pressures from the street. What will now be useful and illuminating is a drawing out of the significance of such work and the formulation of a broader account in such a way as will aid or provoke new work of both a particular and a comparative nature.

QUESTIONS AND POSSIBILITIES

A recognition of the self-absorbed dimension of government provokes a range of questions: what is the nature of the legitimation engaged in as an internal activity of governance and government? What function does this internal legitimation perform in sustaining rulers? What is the relation between internal legitimation and the

---

30 Beetham and Lord, *Legitimacy and the European Union*, p. 12: 'Like any other political body exercising jurisdiction, international institutions require justification in terms of the purposes or ends they serve, which cannot be met by other means, in this case by nation states themselves, or at the individual state level. A continuing ability to meet these purposes, therefore, would seem to be an important condition for the legitimacy of their authority. Yet such justifications rarely percolate out beyond a narrow elite group; nor do they need to, it could be argued, since these institutions are not dependent on the cooperation of a wider public to effect their purposes.'

31 Paul Binski, *Westminster Abbey and the Plantagenets* (New Haven, Yale University Press, 1995); Peter Burke, *The Fabrication of Louis XIV* (New Haven, Yale University Press, 1992); Paul Strohm, *England's Empty Throne: Usurpation and the Language of Legitimation, 1399–1422* (London, Yale University Press, 1998).

32 Lawrence J. Vale, *Architecture, Power and National Identity* (New Haven, Yale University Press, 1992).

33 Guiseppe Di Palma, 'Legitimation from the Top to Civil Society: Politico-Cultural Change in Eastern Europe', *World Politics* 44, 1 (October 1991); Holmes, *The End of Communist Power*; Maria Markus, 'Overt and Covert Modes of Legitimation in East European Societies' in T. H. Rigby and Ference Feher (eds.), *Political Legitimation in Communist States* (London, Macmillan, 1982).

34 Binski, *Westminster Abbey and the Plantagenets*, p. 1.

legitimation of rulers with reference to citizens, voters, and other external ruled or regulated persons? What is the relationship between
the particular form of legitimation pursued, and other features of
the disposition of the resources (time, energy, funds, personnel) of
government? What is the causal and taxonomic character of the
relation between legitimation and the manner of rule, the distribution of power, and the manner of regulation? What comparisons
and contrasts can be identified between legitimation within government, and within the broader activity of governance? It will
not be possible to answer all or even most of these questions. But
raising them broadens the scope of enquiry into government, and
raises the possibility of a more richly dimensional account of it.

OBJECTIONS

Several objections are immediately possible to the depiction of government as a characteristically self-legitimating occupation, or to
the paying of serious academic attention to that activity. Legitimation within government, it might be argued, is a private game. Like
ear lobes, its existence cannot be denied, but it is epiphenomenal
or functionless. Existence is not to be equated with significance or
importance. What matters are the outputs of government, and the
quality of the relationship between rulers and ruled, representatives
and citizens. Carl Friedrich saw no problems in simply dismissing
the whole enterprise: 'if one stresses the objective fact of conformity
of conduct, as we have done, the complexity of human motivation in
adopting such conforming behaviour can be left aside'.[35] Alternatively, it can be objected that legitimation is no more than the dress
that power wears. There are two answers to this charge. First, the
behaviour of government is inherently interesting as a major form
of human behaviour. To social scientists, whatever people spend
time doing is of interest. And whether or not legitimation appears
important to observers, governmental actors appear to treat it very
seriously. The attempt to explain away this attention to legitimation ends up by reinstating what it tries to dismiss. David Easton
many years ago tried to dismiss legitimation as the result of habit or

[35] Carl J. Friedrich, 'Political Leadership and the Problem of Charismatic Power', *The
Journal of Politics* 23 (1961), 3–24, p. 12.

inertia: 'The reliance on legitimacy as a source of diffuse support may have a peculiar result. So ingrained may it become in some systems, that we may suspect that it gives birth to a psychological need to find some leaders and structures in which to believe. If so, belief in legitimacy may become an autonomous goal for the members of a system.'[36] But if legitimation were not already a need, why would it be employed or cultivated in the first place? The argument is a bit like saying that people ate food so often that they became habituated to it, which explains why they continue to do so. Far from being mere trappings or even mere instruments for deceiving the masses, legitimation appears to provide for rulers goods that are valued in themselves. As Inis Claude nicely put it, 'the lovers of naked power are far less typical than those who aspire to clothe themselves in the mantle of legitimate authority; emperors may be nude, but they do not like to be so, to think themselves so, or to be so regarded'.[37] Second, the allocation of resources, energy, time by government is likely to have consequences for ordinary subjects and citizens.

Another objection is to claim that to concentrate on legitimation within government is to abandon normative assessment. The answer to that charge is the same as that implied in the old joke about the Christmas ties, where the giver of two ties, on being confronted with the recipient wearing one of the new gifts complained 'Oh, so you don't like the other one.' Choosing to study one thing is not necessarily to refuse to study something else as well. Still less is it to pass judgement on the value of doing so. The normative complaint could be further countered by the claim that normative assessment must be empirically informed.

THERE IS MUCH FOR WHICH WEBER CAN BE BLAMED

The confusion between 'legitimacy' as either a resource of government or an aspiration of government, and legitimation as a defining characteristic of government, can be found at the start of

[36] David Easton, *A Systems Analysis of Political Life* (New York, John Wiley and Sons, 1965), p. 309.

[37] Inis L. Claude, Jr, 'Collective Legitimization as a Political Function of the United Nations', *International Organization* 20 (1966), 367–79, p. 368.

the modern discussion in the work of Max Weber, though Weber is not as confused as subsequent discussion has made him seem. Weber speaks both of the actions of rulers and ruled in claiming or denying legitimacy, in other words in engaging in legitimation, and of the character of rule. Thus action 'may be guided by the belief in the existence of a legitimate order'[38] and 'actors may ascribe legitimacy to a social order'[39] whilst at the same time 'legitimacy' can be treated as a characteristic of a social order.[40] There is a further confusion, or at least ambiguity, in that sometimes Weber speaks of legitimation as a feature of the relations between people, and, at others, as a feature of relations between systems or institutions.[41] The trap into which subsequent commentators have fallen is to assume that, since Weber spoke of the ascription of legitimacy and of belief in legitimacy, the historian or political scientist could most profitably proceed by asking the same questions as did rulers and their subjects and supporters: 'Is this regime legitimate, does it possess legitimacy?' Weber identified this mistake in his criticisms of Rudolph Stammler for failing to distinguish between the normative and the empirical.[42] The error is illustrated if the question is asked of a specific form of legitimation. It would occur to few contemporary observers to ask, 'Does the king really enjoy divine authorisation, is he really possessed of divine right?' Yet as soon as the method of legitimation moves from the pre-modern form of divine right to the modern form of contract and consent, it is assumed that, because words are used, the things to which they refer must be real, and observable and testable by third parties. We no longer accept the ontological proof of the existence of God, but are happy to accept ontological proofs of the existence of legitimacy, or justice, or authority.

It is possible to go too far in the opposite direction. The ironist as described by Richard Rorty, 'thinks that the occurrence of a term like "just" or "scientific" or "rational" in the final vocabulary of the day is no reason to think that Socratic enquiry into the essence

---

[38] Weber, *Economy and Society*, p. 31.

[39] Ibid., p. 36.

[40] Ibid., p. 33.

[41] Peter M. Blau, 'Critical Remarks on Weber's Theory of Authority', *American Political Science Review* 57, 2 (June 1963), 305–16, p. 307.

[42] Weber, *Economy and Society*, p. 32.

of justice or science or rationality will take one much beyond the language games of one's time'.[43] But 'the language games of one's time' should not be dismissed as trivial. They are engaged in with serious and benign intent by many who seek thereby to advance the happiness of humanity or the justice with which it arranges its affairs. Whether one dismisses such activity as a contingent game or, alternatively, sees it as a modern version of theological disputation, one is left with its clear embedded presence as a major and ubiquitous feature of human life. One may say that its aims rest on a misconception, but one cannot say that the observation of its importance rests on a misconception, since it is a clearly real and perennial feature of that contingent activity summarised as human life.

DEFENDING WEBER

The objection frequently made to Weber's discussion of legitimacy, that he is saying that legitimacy exists when people believe it exists,[44] is answered by first acknowledging and then explaining the accusation. There are not two separate things, 'legitimacy' and 'belief in legitimacy'. 'Legitimacy' is a fiction, a metaphor which we employ to describe circumstances where people accept the claims made by rulers. Beliefs, in this sense, are not evidence of some further, distinct phenomenon called legitimacy, they are what we are describing when we say things such as 'the regime is legitimate' or 'the regime enjoys legitimacy'. So if we ask whether a regime is legitimate, historically or empirically what that question must mean is 'is the regime legitimated?' 'Are there actions which we can observe or infer which constitute legitimation?' Legitimation, as an activity, in other words, rather than the metaphorical condition or property of legitimacy, is what empirical or historical, as opposed to normative, social science is concerned with. The phrase 'as opposed to normative' is of course crucial. The elaboration of criteria by which the observer recommends the normative appraisal of

---

[43] Richard Rorty, *Contingency, Irony and Solidarity* (Cambridge, Cambridge University Press, 1989), pp. 74–5.

[44] This is a frequent charge, of which David Beetham's is the most recent restatement. Beetham, *The Legitimation of Power*, pp. 8–13. But see also Anthony Giddens, *Studies in Social and Political Theory* (London, Hutchinson, 1979), p. 92, and Barker, *Political Legitimacy and the State*, pp. 56–60.

regimes is an inherent aspect of political science. But it is also a
distinct and different one from the empirical or historical study of
how government is carried on.

There are passages where Weber leaves less room for confusion.
In the essay 'Politics as a Vocation' he writes that the state is that
'human community that (successfully) claims the *monopoly of the legitimate use of physical force* within a given territory'.[45] The claim is what
characterises the human institutions called states, in other words,
not the possession of some abstract quality called legitimacy. This
is highlighted by a frequent complaint made against Weber, that
he provided no conception of illegitimacy. Melvin Richter, for example, complains that Weber was not interested in, and did not
have place in his schema, for a concept of illegitimacy. This is compared with those writers, including Tocqueville, who developed
arguments whereby to call in question the acceptability of the rule
of Napoleon.[46] But the question of states seeking for some property
called legitimacy in order to succeed or survive no more arises than
does the question of elephants seeking mammalian status. Mammals is one of the things that elephants are, and the most one can ask
are questions of degree: not 'is it a warm blooded quadruped that
suckles its young?', but 'how many young?' Similarly with states,
as Peter Stillman, whilst still employing the concept of legitimacy,
insists, it is a matter of degree.[47] Legitimation is not a condition of
the success of rulers so much as a characteristic of the phenomenon
of being a ruler. In that sense, an unlegitimated state is a contradiction in terms, whatever further judgements may be made about the
political character and moral status of the regime. Arthur Vidich
and Ronald Glassman suggest that much of the ancient world was
'illegitimate', and give as examples of non-legitimate regimes,
'Rome's entire political history from Augustus to Claudius and
beyond to the fall of Rome'; Italian cities during 'almost the entire period of the Renaissance'; and the contemporary regimes
where 'almost the entire Third World is ruled by military regimes,

---

[45] 'Politics as a Vocation' in Mills and Gerth (eds.), *From Max Weber*, p. 78. Italics in the
original.
[46] Melvin Richter, 'Towards a Concept of Political Illegitimacy: Bonapartist Dictatorship
and Democratic Legitimacy', *Political Theory* 10, 2 (May 1982), 185–214.
[47] So Peter Stillman, while still employing the concept of legitimacy, insists that it is a matter
of degree. Stillman, 'The Concept of Legitimacy'.

dictatorships, or fragile coalitions which exist under conditions of extreme instability'.[48] As an empirical or historical observation, it is rather like saying that half of all sparrows are essentially flightless. It can be sustained as a normative judgement, but not helpfully as an historical or empirical one. States depend on successful legitimation only in the sense that mammals depend upon suckling their young. If they lacked that characteristic, mammals would not survive. But neither would creatures which lacked that characteristic be mammals. This is the inverse of the point made by Eugene Huskey in a discussion of Mancur Olson's work, 'Doesn't your argument rest on the tautology that a government falls because a government ceases to be a government?'[49] Since the claim to legitimacy is one of the characteristics of government, to ask is the government legitimate can be tautologous. To ask in what way, and with what success, does it claim legitimacy, is by contrast an appropriate question. Legitimation is to beliefs about government what worship is to beliefs about God. It is an observable human activity, whose study does not require any judgement about moral worth or, in the religious analogy, theological truth.[50]

SOCIAL SCIENCE AND THE SUBJECT MATTER OF SOCIAL SCIENCE

The sociological or historical study of legitimation can learn a lesson from the fact of the normative study of legitimacy. The normative study is, for the sociologist or the historian, an instance of human conduct, one of the many ways in which people act politically. But the historical or sociological examination is democratically empirical, and does not imagine that an activity which is carried on with great skill by a few is not carried on elsewhere

---

[48] Arthur J. Vidich and Ronald M. Glassman, 'Introduction' in Vidich and Glassman (eds.), *Conflict and Control: Challenges to Legitimacy of Modern Governments*, 9–14 (London, Sage, 1979), p. 13.

[49] Eugene Huskey, 'Comment on "The Logic of Collective Action in Soviet-type Societies"', *Journal of Soviet Nationalities* 1 (Summer 1990), p. 28.

[50] Roger Scruton comments that 'From the Norman Conquest to the contemporary reactions to trade-union power, the concept of legitimacy has governed political practice, and whether or not there is any reality which corresponds to this concept is a question that may be put aside as of no political (although of great philosophical) significance' Roger Scruton, *The Meaning of Conservatism* (Harmondsworth: Penguin, 1980), p. 29.

as well, even if with different intensity or less sophistication. The moral claims and judgements which political philosophers and normative theorists make are not their monopoly. Rulers and subjects engage in a form of the same activity, and for the sociologist or the historian or the political scientist, all are instances of political conduct, and of a form of conduct which is one of the universal and characteristic features of government and of politics. Nor are social scientists isolated from the world they study: their judgements are part of it. They immediately add to the body of argument, and quite possibly of legitimation, which they aim only to study. One justification for their existence and work is that they do just that, so that 'the relation of social scientific and lay discourses may strive towards attaining an overt dialogue of potentially emancipatory, demystifying critique'.[51] Not only is there 'a continuum, in other words, between the debates among political actors and publics, and the analytical concerns of political scientists',[52] but in an important sense all are versions of the same activity.

LEGITIMATION AND LEGITIMACY

A useful working distinction, despite this double role of the normative political scientist as both subject and object, can be made between legitimacy as an ascribed attribute, and legitimation, the action of ascribing. Each conception has its own contribution to make, and the possibilities and limitations of each need to be recognised. Whilst normative discussions of legitimacy are an important part of refining the moral language of politics, they have less to contribute to an understanding of government, and can mislead the expectations of those who wish to analyse rulers or regimes

[51] David Campbell, 'Truth Claims and Value-Freedom in the Treatment of Legitimacy: The Case of Weber', *Journal of Law and Society* 13, 2 (Summer 1986), 207–24, p. 221. 'If actors' beliefs are shown by social explanation to contain mistakes, then these must be criticised by any social science striving for adequacy to its subject matter. Some evaluation will inevitably enter into any account of those beliefs; either ideologically in the form of an obscured evaluation or potentially openly. These beliefs are capable of being reflexively examined by those who profess them, and the relation of social scientific and lay discourses may strive towards attaining an overt dialogue of potentially emancipatory, demystifying critique.'

[52] Beetham and Lord, *Legitimacy and the European Union*, p. 2.

of which they may disapprove. Judgmental social science has an important place, but it also has its limits. Enquiries as to whether or not a regime is legitimate too easily conclude with a judgement which has either no explanatory future, or no descriptive content. If we have to wait, like litigants in court, to hear the judgement of scholars on whether or not a regime is legitimate, then whatever quality it is that the court of political science is awarding cannot have been of very much significance if the only sign of its existence is its attribution by observers, and if nothing of any consequence flows from that attribution. We learn nothing more by the judgement than that the regime was, or was not, legitimate. Everything else we know about it remains unchanged. On the other hand, an enquiry into the ways a regime legitimates itself and the counter-legitimations which are to be found amongst its opponents can reveal political actions which both constitute and cause a particular outcome in the conduct and character of government.

One simple and already available means of underlining the distinctions involved is to reserve the terms 'legitimacy' and 'legitimate', respectively descriptive of an object and of the property of an object, to normative enquiry, and to use the term 'legitimation' for the discussion of observable human activity. Such a distinction between action and property has been briefly suggested by François Bourricaud.[53] The difference is between an argument about how we ought to behave, and a description of expressions of 'oughtness' as a feature of political life. Frequently the terms 'legitimacy' and 'legitimation' are used in the course of a single discussion, and in a way that implies that all that is involved is a shift of vantage point. But much more than this is involved in shifting from the action of legitimation to the 'product' or 'property' of legitimacy, and the choice of terms involves a fundamental choice of conceptualisation. It is the argument of this book that legitimation is a distinct and valuable concept, and that once it has been distinguished from other concepts which do different work, a theory of legitimation is possible which solves problems which have held up the study of politics and government, and which facilitates more fruitful investigation in future.

[53] François Bourricaud, 'Legitimacy and Legitimation', *Current Sociology* 35, 2 (1987), 57–67, p. 57.

Legitimation is an activity in which rulers engage. They claim that they possess a distinguishing, specific monopoly of the right to rule, of 'legitimacy'. Legitimation is an activity which can be observed, it is something that people do, just as they challenge legitimation. On the other hand 'legitimacy', the thing claimed, is from the point of view of the observer not a phenomenon that can be observed. We do not, in other words, need to treat as real objects the alleged ends of political argument, of rhetoric, of the justificatory side of political contest. To talk of legitimation is to talk of something that people do, a contest between rulers and their opponents, or between competing sides in a civil war, a dynastic conflict, or the politics of coups or insurrections. It is to remain outside the activity, describing and analysing it. To talk of 'legitimacy', on the other hand, is to actualise what may be actual to the participants, but is to the observer simply a metaphor or hypothetical state or abbreviation employed by those whom she studies.

The huge amount of energy that rulers put into legitimation can be observed. Legitimation in this sense is neither a cause nor a condition of government, but a defining component. 'Defining' in the sense that government nowhere occurs without it because without that component, though not that component alone, it is not government at all. When David Beetham and Christopher Lord write that regime 'crises typically occur when a significant deficit in the source of authority and its validating beliefs is compounded by performance failure, and leads to the active withdrawal of consent on the part of those qualified to give it',[54] it can be replied that crises do not occur as a result of those events, but rather the confluence of those events is what a crisis is. The crisis is not some further event caused by the listed events, but is constituted by them. Crises or erosions of legitimacy do not cause crises or erosions of government. They are a constituent part of what crises or erosions of government are. Since legitimation is a normal part of government, it is looking at the wrong question to ask 'Is this society legitimate?'[55]

---

[54] Beetham and Lord, *Legitimacy and the European Union*, p. 10.
[55] This is a similar point, though arising from a different argument, to that made by Richard Rorty when he writes of a shift in understanding 'that makes it impossible to ask the question "Is ours a moral society?"', Richard Rorty, *Contingency, Irony and Solidarity* (Cambridge, Cambridge University Press, 1989), p. 59.

The question to be asked is the different one, 'In what way does legitimation take place in this society?' There will not be a single answer.[56]

Whilst everyone makes ethical or moral judgements on rulers, legitimation has a proper and useful role as a non-normative term used to describe the expression of claims by a particular state or group of rulers. At the extreme and uncongenial end of the spectrum it would make perfect sense to talk of the Pol Pot regime in Cambodia before its displacement by Vietnam, or the military dictatorship of SLORC and its successors in Burma, as legitimating themselves or as engaging in legitimation in that they spent time, effort, and resources on expressing, in a variety of ways, claims about their 'legitimacy'. The regime's empirical or historical actions of legitimation are distinct from any normative assessment which may be made of them by political scientists or historians. Conversely, the fact that we might feel respect for the benevolent intentions or responsible policies of a regime has no simple or direct consequences for the way in which we give an account of its legitimating actions.

A MORATORIUM ON THE USE OF 'LEGITIMACY'?

Although the term 'legitimacy' unavoidably occurs in the following chapters, there would have been a great advantage in not using it at all. There could even be a case for arguing that, at least for a while, the word should be put in storage, and that it would be helpful to make a working assumption that there is no such thing as legitimacy, any more than there are 'power', 'honour', or 'beauty'. François Bourricaud has argued pretty much this, writing that the idea of a legitimate, or an illegitimate, society 'has no meaning'.[57] It could be argued that the words are metaphors used to describe relations between people and the actions people take by treating beliefs as if they were responses to real objects or phenomena. The metaphors are a useful fiction, derived from the way in which people do in fact speak, and

[56] As I have already argued in Barker, 'Legitimacy: The Identity of the Accused'
[57] Bourricaud, 'Legitimacy and Legitimation', p. 67.

advancing understanding by empathising with the actions being described.[58]

So it could be helpful, if only to shift our point of vision, to insist that 'legitimacy' does not exist as a feasible subject of empirical or historical enquiry, in the same sense that God does not exist as a possible subject for social scientific study. We need to speak of both legitimacy and God when describing the actions of people engaged in politics and religion, but when we do so, we are describing their actions and language, not any independent phenomenon, or independent aspect of the institutions they have created or seek to create, nor any independent being in relation to whom they stand. So in the argument which follows, when I unavoidably use the terms 'legitimacy' and 'legitimate government', I am not thereby making any judgement about the truth of such claims by rulers, nor of the moral worth of the character which they present either to themselves or to their subjects. It is the act of justification or authorisation which is being described, not the phenomena, character, or principles which are invoked as part of that action.

Expressions of 'oughtness' are the raw material with which I am working not in order to establish a set of recommendations which all reasonable or fully informed people should follow, but as a feature of the political conduct which I attempt to describe. As such they are as varied as expressions of loyalty or hostility, association or aversion in religion, or football, or opera. And whilst almost everyone believes theirs is the right answer to the question of why and when rulers should be obeyed, and I, like anyone else, have views about obligation, authority, politics, citizenship, and government, I am not setting out here to advance them. I deal with legitimation because it and the disputes over it are a central feature of government and politics, not because I am a participant in a debate about oughtness or obligation. I am not turning my back on those debates save in the sense that to choose to do one thing is to choose not to do another. They are important debates

---

[58] The point has been made from a different angle by the anthropologist David Kertzer: 'Authority, the belief that a person has the right to exercise influence over others' behaviour, is itself an abstraction, and people can conceive of who has authority and who has not only through symbols and rituals', David L. Kertzer, *Ritual, Politics, and Power* (New Haven and London, Yale University Press, 1988), p. 24.

conducted with great skill. But I am not setting out here to make a contribution to them, but to other discussions.

It may be objected that to set aside legitimacy as a word or a concept which refers to anything identifiable, or which performs any helpful or illuminating function, is to ignore a great many events where the term is applied, and where it seems an appropriate term. Does it not make sense to say that East European communist regimes lost legitimacy between 1989 and 1991? Is there not some sense in saying that the European Union lacks legitimacy? My provisional answer to this question and this objection is that clearly events of great importance were occurring, and that the use of the term legitimacy draws attention to those events. But it can also obscure them. What additional accounts are available or might be constructed, I will return to in later chapters.

THE MISTAKE OF ORTHODOXY

Moratoriums have their attractions, and one response to the variety of terms and meanings would be to establish coherence and simplicity by criticising all but those uses which could be marshalled within a single concept, or replacing them all with such a concept. But the prohibition of usage, though briefly illuminating as a thought experiment, is not the best way forward. Nor is a search for orthodoxy, for the 'correct' meaning of legitimation and legitimacy, the best way to proceed. The terms 'legitimacy', 'legitimation', and 'legitimate' do not refer to some single and uncontentious objective reality. Rather they are used to construct a network of related but distinct descriptions of government and politics. Although I criticise some of the existing usages, it is not my intention to establish orthodoxy, but rather to point to aspects of politics and governments which, despite the profusion, have been ignored or insufficiently described in existing work. This will involve talking about a particular kind of legitimation, and in establishing space for such usage the argument may seem to cut other usages out of the way. That may be a ground-clearing convenience, but it is not in the end intended to reduce the variety of species. The purpose is not to arrive at a 'correct' usage of legitimation, far less to establish what legitimation 'really is'. Writers who have used the terms 'legitimacy' and 'legitimation' have sometimes attempted to do this,[59] but such a search for true meaning does not advance understanding very much. It is not my purpose, which is simply to begin the identification of what appears to be a central and characterising activity of government, to which existing work pays insufficient attention.

The approach outlined in the following pages to some extent shares the view of the world advanced by post-modern theory. It is sceptical of grand and simple explanations or categorisations; it doubts the usefulness or closeness to human experience of the isolation of factors, causes, and resources which modernism appears to permit; it accepts the need for a general, even universal setting out of the possible elements of human government and politics – but it expects that the character and experience of any actually observable governed community will be in many ways unique, and that these unique aspects will frequently be central to the political experience so described. The account proposed is symbiotic rather than, in a one-directional manner, causal or mechanical. This opens up many possibilities, though not possibilities of easy laws, generalisations, or predictions.

If politics is to be properly seen as neither unrooted thought nor mindless behaviour, cultural conceptions such as legitimation are essential. Politics as conduct must be seen as the continual creation, maintenance, erosion, and contestation of government. For that reason I have conceptualised legitimation as an active, contested political process, rather than legitimacy as an abstract political resource. Since it is an activity, not a property, it involves creation, modification, innovation, and transformation.

Would a different word than 'legitimation' be appropriate? It would not be necessary, since there are already existing terms which serve well enough to draw the outlines of the activity I wish to describe. 'Endogenous legitimation' or 'self-legitimation' draw on the

---

59 For instance, Christel Lane comments critically on Rigby's discussion of self-legitimation within a ruling elite, that it is 'extremely doubtful whether the phenomenon under investigation is still legitimacy, or whether it is perhaps something else, wrongly bestowed with this name'. Christel Lane, 'Legitimacy and Power in the Soviet Union through Socialist Ritual', *British Journal of Political Science* 14 (1984), 219–32, p. 210. David Beetham similarly argues against the view that legitimacy is 'chiefly of consequence for the members of the state apparatus, or the political élite, and has little relevance for the population as a whole'. Beetham, *The Legitimation of Power*, p. 33.

accounts of justification, authorising, whilst at the same time being distinct from, unqualified nouns. They indicate the use of prestige and identification in the service of rulers' justification of themselves, and the articulation of a governing purposes in the cultivation of prestige and self-identification. They may not be perfect terms, but they will do in the way that a completely new word, which would conceal the connections with existing descriptions and existing usage, would not.

CHAPTER 2

Legitimating identities

WHAT THIS BOOK IS ABOUT: THEMES AND ARGUMENT

It is now possible to return to the coronation of Napoleon, and to state the position which this book attempts to argue and illustrate. I shall set out the points of the argument in a fairly dogmatic manner, not on the assumption that they will thereby be more convincing, but in order that the account given in the book should be clear, and that there are no consciously or deliberately hidden assumptions in the discussion.

Endogenous or self-legitimation is a characteristic activity of government

It is an activity, which can be observed and which comprises all those actions which rulers, but not only rulers, take to insist on or demonstrate, as much to themselves as to others, that they are justified in the pattern of actions that they follow. Self-legitimation is an inherent and characterising activity of government, just as worship is one of the characterising activities of religion, or singing one of the characterising features of choral music. It may of course characterise other activities also, but in different ways. The self-legitimation of rulers is part of the activity of ruling, and as such contributes to both constituting it and defining it. There will be many views about the value or acceptability of the legitimation conducted by different rulers, just as there will be many views about religious doctrine and ritual, or musical quality. Such disputes are an endemic accompaniment of such activities.

Legitimation is hierarchically pursued

The rituals of rule, which are most commonly presented as part of the public face of government, are just as much a part of its private face. Rulers legitimate their position and power to themselves and to their immediate staff, who are their immediate mirrors, at least as much as they do to the mass of those whom they govern and whose support in votes, taxes, and time and effort they cultivate. Those who practise legitimation most do so in relation to their own referential hinterland,[1] rather than to the wider community. Legitimation is an activity conducted in the first place within groups, and only secondarily between them. It is the recognition of this in Weber's account of legitimation which enables Bryan Turner to describe it as 'ruler-centred'.[2]

Self, as Erving Goffman has put it, may be presented in everyday life.[3] But it is not in the everyday life of everyday people alone that the presentation of self takes place. Rulers cultivate their dramatic personalities just as does everyone else, and self is presented in the signing of treaties just as much as in the buying of bread and marmalade. Everyday life is not always mundane. To invert the point, but to make the same observation, everyday life goes on at all levels and in all circumstances. It is lived by presidents and prime ministers just as it is by priests and plumbers. Goffman's observations, however, describe the presentation of self as a functional form of social communication. It has another function, which is the self-knowledge and self-justification of the actor.

People, not laws or commands, rulers, not regimes are legitimated

I shall argue that the concepts of identity and identification provide a key to the understanding of legitimation and vice versa.

---

[1] Pierre Muller and Bruno Jobert have employed the notion of the 'référentiel' to describe such a representation of the task and structure one is engaged with and one's own place within it. Bruno Jobert and Pierre Muller, *L'État en action: politiques publiques et corporatismes* (Paris, Presses Universitaires de France, 1987).

[2] Bryan S. Turner, 'Nietzsche, Weber, and the Devaluation of Politics: The Problem of State Legitimacy', *Sociological Review* 30 (1982), pp. 367–91, p. 370: 'Since Weber's theory of legitimacy is rooted in the nature of normative commands and claims on political resources, his construction of the legitimacy problem was skewed towards the ruler rather than to the ruled.'

[3] E. Goffman, *The Presentation of Self in Everyday Life* (New York, Doubleday, 1959).

Harold Laski argued that it was false to assume that 'the pursuit
of evil can be made good by the character of the performer'.[4] But
whilst that is a sound argument within normative political science,
the precise opposite may occur in government and politics as empirically or historically observed. Commands are justified not only
because their content is claimed to be good, or wise, or advanta-
geous, but because of an identification between the person giving
the command and some particular quality, image, or ideal. Good
commands are commands issued by good people, admirable rules
the instructions of admirable rulers. This is not to reject Laski's
moral point, but it is to suggest that it is not an adequate empirical
or historical description of how government works.

Legitimation is principally a statement about a person issuing
an instruction, making a demand, or stating or implying a wish. It
is a claim or expression made by or on behalf of that person to assert the special and distinctive identity which that person possesses,
which identity justifies or authorises or legitimates the command
by legitimating the person issuing it. It is in the first place persons not systems, rulers not regimes, who are legitimated. If you
do not trust someone, or recognise them, or yourself, as having
a particular identity, no argument or judicial case for legitimacy
will change things. This trust of persons can extend to categories
of person, so that when in the seventeenth century there was a
widening acceptance of the results of scientific enquiry,[5] or in the
late twentieth century a growing scepticism, the process involved
a perception not of the methods of enquiry or of the institutions
carrying them out, but of the people doing the investigation. In
each case the judgement was not on science, but on scientists. Similarly, it is more common to hear calls for 'no bishop, no king', than
to receive a demand for the ending of monarchy and episcopacy.
The process here described is similar to that involved in personal
affection, or a taste in music or food. In none of these cases is affection, enjoyment, or loyalty the result of rational appraisal from a
distance. They arise from an actual experience, direct, indirect, or
imagined of a person, a piece of music, a type of food, or an image
or perception of them.

[4] H. J. Laski, *Studies in the Problem of Sovereignty*, quoted in David Nicholls, *The Pluralist State:
   The Political Ideas of J. N. Figgis and His Contemporaries* 2nd edn (London, 1994), p. 47.
[5] Steven Shapin, *The Scientific Revolution* (Chicago, Chicago University Press, 1996).

Weber envisaged a progression from charismatic to legal rational legitimation as charisma was bureaucratised. But there was a contrast or at least a tension between his theoretical account of the progress of history and his more particular observations about the course of contemporary politics.[6] There was also, as Peter Blau has pointed out, a tension between his theoretical and his historical observations. 'When he presents his abstract definitions, he seems to refer to authority in interpersonal relations. In his analysis of empirical situations, on the other hand, he is concerned with political systems or institutions, such as feudalism.'[7] This tension, between an account of structures and circumstances, and an account of individual action, is inherent in social science, and progress takes, amongst many other forms, a continual correction of an undue neglect of one or an undue dominance of the other. One of the contributions of rational choice theory within political science has been a reassertion of the importance of individual agency, even if it has at the same time been insufficiently sensitive to the individuality of individuals.

The legitimation of persons rather than of sets of constitutional arrangements is most obvious in the case of personal rule. Monarchs, revolutionary leaders, rulers who in one way or another claim divine authority, clearly are making statements about themselves. But rulers in constitutional or democratic systems too legitimate themselves by describing themselves, rather than the systems within which they work. As Juan Linz comments, 'the legitimacy of a democratic regime rests on the belief in the right of those legally elevated to authority to issue certain types of commands, to expect obedience, and to enforce them'.[8] To say one is the people's choice is to make a statement in the first place about oneself, not about the people.

However much allegiance may be given to the rule of law or the constitution or due process, law in concrete instances is always someone's command. Similarly, the subject of legitimation is specific and personal, rather than abstract or structural. Legitimation is carried out by the king in one or other of his two bodies,

---

[6] D. Beetham, *Max Weber and the Theory of Modern Politics* (London, George Allen and Unwin, 1974).

[7] Peter M. Blau, 'Critical Remarks on Weber's Theory of Authority', *American Political Science Review* 57, 2 (June 1963), 305 16, p. 307.

[8] Juan J. Linz, *The Breakdown of Democracratic Regimes: Crisis, Breakdown, and Reequilibration* (Baltimore, Johns Hopkins University Press, 1978), p. 17.

not by monarchy. It is individuals, or rather the public roles of individuals which is all we can ever deal with in politics anyway, who are legitimated, not institutions. Free-range public claims and protests, as against battery questionnaires, are generally attached to identified people, not to institutions. What is striking is how universally legitimation focusses on persons rather than on principles or processes. Even when institutions are formally the focus of a legitimation claim, the institution is personalised: not the EU commission, but 'those bureaucrats in Brussels'; not federal agencies, but east coast liberals.

There is an in-built disposition against accepting this view, or an in-built disposition in favour of seeing institutions and procedures, rather than persons, as legitimated, in a democratic, contractual approach to government. It can be objected, from this vantage point, that to depict legitimation as justifying systems, sets of rules, or simply an abstract concept such as power, is to depersonalise it, and facilitate a rational, contractarian conception.[9] If it is hoped that government can be a matter of consent, rules, and agreed procedures, then it is those rules, rather than the persons who employ, or circumvent them, which are to be the focus of legitimation. To treat legitimation as the justification of persons issuing commands is, by contrast, to employ an elitist perspective, which undermines democratic principles of representation and accountability. If individuals exercise authority, and the focus is on what the command giver says and does, then so too is the focus on the ruler, rather than on the democratic procedures of which he is the agent, or which constrain him. A partial answer to this charge is that to analyse a phenomenon is not to condone it, and if one opposes it, analysis is a useful basis for remedy.

Legitimation and identification

Legitimation and identification are inextricably linked. Each is to be understood in terms of the other. The principal way in which

---

[9] David Beetham thus speaks of the legitimation of power, and though he discusses also the government of persons, his rational contractarian approach sits more easily with his discussion of systems. David Beetham, *The Legitimation of Power* (London, Macmillan, 1991).

people issuing commands are legitimated is by their being identified as special, marked by particular qualities, set apart from other people. When rulers legitimate themselves, they give an account of who they are, in writing, in images, in more or less ceremonial actions and practices. The action both creates and expresses the identity. The identity at one and the same time legitimates the person, and is confirmed by the person's manner of expressing it. Legitimation and identification are in that sense dimensions of an inextricably intermeshed activity or pattern of activities. At the same time, identification between rulers and the people to whom the commands are issued serves to legitimate compliance with commands. Uncongenial commands from 'our people' can be more acceptable than congenial commands from 'foreigners' or those who are 'not one of us'. Identification is the key to understanding legitimation, and legitimation one of the principal functions of identification. Each concept is incomplete in itself – brought together they become a powerful form of explanation. This conceptualisation of identification and legitimation gets beyond the limitations both of 'legitimacy as a resource' and of the brick wall which rational choice theory finds itself confronting in the matter. Identification has come to be treated as a major element in politics. What has been less attended to is that it is a major element in government. Nor need interest and identity be juxtaposed. It is not necessary to insist that we 'act, not in defence of our interests, but in defence of our identity'.[10] Each is constructed in terms of the other, and each is necessary to make the other comprehensible.[11]

Two meanings of identification

The term identification has two meanings, both of which are part of what is being described here. I identify myself in the sense of having a sense of my own identity. But I identify with those who seem to me to share with me some characteristic which I value. The two forms of identification relate to and sustain each other. The

[10] Erik Ringmar, *Identity, Interest and Action: A Cultural Explanation of Sweden's Intervention in the Thirty Years War* (Cambridge, Cambridge University Press, 1996), p. 4.
[11] Rodney Barker, 'Hooks and Hands, Interests and Enemies: Political Thinking as Political Action', *Political Studies* 48, 2, Special Issue (2000).

existence of prestigious others with whom I can identify strengthens
my sense of my own identity and its worth. My sense of myself as
having a particular identity strengthens my identification of my self
with others whom I see as similar.[12]

Identification and legitimation are significant activities

This argument depends upon or is at least sustained by and associated with the argument that people take identification and legitimation very seriously, and that these are political activities of the
highest importance. They, and politics and government, are not
properly understood if they are seen as auxiliary, epiphenomenal,
or means simply to other ends. Rulers spend a great deal of time, effort, and resources on activities which have no immediate material
function but are elements in a culture of legitimation. Democratic
empiricism[13] may oblige us to take seriously the apparently irrational rituals of popular politics; aristocratic empiricism makes even
greater claims.

Enemies and the common people

The converse of the limited referential community of elite legitimation is the role played by the conception of enemies. Enemies
are necessary to identification, since by saying who it is not, an
individual, community, or group marks out its boundaries more
clearly. There is a polarity here. The common people are in a sense
less part of the referential community of the elite than are enemies.

Legitimation enables people to obey and to command

Legitimation is a means of achieving ethical coherence, of matching
the account given of a person's identity to others of their actions.
If a person is to act in a manner which is markedly different from

---

[12] Charles Taylor, following Hegel, has spoken of 'recognition' in describing some of what I
am talking about here. Charles Taylor, *Multiculturalism: Examining The Politics of Recognition*,
ed. and with Introduction by Amy Gutman, 2nd edn (Princeton, Princeton University
Press, 1994).
[13] Barker, 'Hooks and Hands, Interests and Enemies', p. 228.

the actions of other people, the created, cultivated, or sustained identity must in its turn be distinctive. Otherwise the actions, in this case those of governing, are incoherent and random, lacking the patterned correspondence with each other which is familiar or expected in that particular society. Karl Deutsch, whilst using the term in a sense at one remove from that employed here, contributes to the same understanding when he comments that legitimacy 'is the expectation of long-run compatibility of a personal or social goal, role, or value with other salient goals, roles, or values which are critical for the maintenance of the personality of the actor, or of the survival and cohesion of the social group'.[14] Thomas Luckman comments that 'legitimation is making sense of power . . . to those who exercise power; to those who are subject to the exercise of power; or to both'.[15] A similar point is made by Peter Berger. Legitimations are 'answers to any questions about the "why" of institutional arrangements' and as such are just as necessary to those in charge of such arrangements as to those arranged by them.[16]

But if legitimation assists people to obey, it is even more important in assisting people to rule, in justifying their rule and making it coherent *for them*. Weber talks of the need for ethical meaning or justification. He argues that 'when a civil servant appears in his office daily at a fixed time, he does not act only on the basis of custom or self-interest which he could disregard if he wanted to' but also because not to do so 'would be abhorrent to his sense of duty'.[17] His description has been heavily influential, but not pervasively so. Otto Hinze sounds uncannily like Weber when he writes that 'Man does not live by bread alone; he wants to have a good conscience when he pursues his vital interests.'[18] Joseph Bensman goes so far as to argue that 'the self-justification that is the motivating drive for legitimacy is a particular expression of what for Weber was a deep, metaphysical need: the need for a rational meaning of the

---

[14] Karl Deutsch, 'The Commitment of National Legitimacy Symbols as a Verification Technique', *The Journal of Conflict Resolution* 7, 3 (September 1963), 360–9, p. 362.
[15] Thomas Luckman, 'Comments on Legitimation', *Current Sociology* 35, 2 (1987), 109–17.
[16] Peter L. Berger, *The Sacred Canopy: Elements of a Sociological Theory of Religion* (Garden City, NY, Doubleday, 1967), pp. 29, 31.
[17] Max Weber, *Economy and Society*, Guenther Roth and Claus Wittich (eds.), 2 vols. (London, University of California Press, 1978), p. 31.
[18] F. Gilbert (ed.), *The Historical Essays of Otto Hintze* (New York, Oxford University Press, 1975), p. 94.

cosmos, the world, and for man's place in it. It includes the need
for an ethical interpretation of the world.'[19] The studies of Pierre
Bourdieu of what he terms the 'state elite' in contemporary France
follow Weber's account of the need for self-justification closely, and
when Bourdieu writes that 'No power can be satisfied with existing
just as power, that is, as brute force, entirely devoid of justification –
in a word, arbitrary – and it must thus justify its existence',[20] the
intellectual lineage is clear.

Picking up a clue from Weber: the correspondence of types of rule and types of legitimation

The formation of institutional identities both justifies the exercise
of power and describes the ways and ends of its use. The point was
most succinctly made by Weber: 'according to the kind of legitimacy
which is claimed, the type of obedience, the kind of administrative
staff developed to guarantee it, and the mode of exercising authority, will all differ fundamentally',[21] i.e. the relationship is reciprocal
and organic, rather than in any simple sense causal. The role of
legitimating identification is not a unique feature of 'ceremonial'
or 'traditional' societies, though its manner will differ with other
aspects of government. This relationship between legitimation and
other features of rule can be detected in representative regimes and
autocracies alike.[22] The nature of this correspondence lies beyond
the scope of this book, save to argue that there is a reciprocal relation between legitimation and other aspects of rule. Each sustains

---

[19] Joseph Bensman, 'Max Weber's Concept of Legitimacy: An Evaluation' in Arthur
J. Vidich and Ronald Glassman (eds.), *Conflict and Control: Challenges to Legitimacy of Modern
Governments* 17–48 (Beverley Hills, Sage, 1979), p. 32.

[20] Pierre Bourdieu, *The State Nobility: Elite Schools in the Field of Power*, trans. Lauretta Clough
(Cambridge, Polity, 1996), p. 265.

[21] Weber, *Economy and Society*, p. 213; cf. the attempt to simplify this relationship by making
it a one-way causal one by C. Matheson, 'Weber and the Classification of Forms of
Legitimacy', *British Journal of Sociology* 2 (1987), 199–215.

[22] 'even in cases where the system of rule is so assured of dominance that its claim to legitimacy plays little or no part in the relationship between rulers and subjects, the mode of
legitimation retains its significance as the basis for the relation of authority between rulers
and administrative staff and for the structure of rule', T. H. Rigby, 'Introduction: Political
Legitimacy, Weber and Communist Mono-organisational Systems' in T. H. Rigby and
Ferenc Féher (eds.), *Political Legitimation in Communist States* (New York, St. Martin's Press,
1982), p. 15.

the other, and since rulers seek for coherence, and for justification which is a form of coherence, this correspondence will always be to some extent deliberately sought and cultivated. This is an important form of rationality: not the matching of internal values to external actions, because there are only external actions of one form or another, but the matching of one action so far as possible with another.

THE SCOPE AND CHARACTER OF A THEORY OF LEGITIMATION

What use is an account of legitimation?

Any account or theory of legitimation is likely to be of little help in either predicting or influencing the course of government and politics. This is so for several reasons. First, the distance between academic theory, however accessible, and actual political circumstances, is frequently considerable. Second, the account which political scientists can give of legitimation will describe the relationships between a number of factors, all of which are likely to sustain and influence one another. In these circumstances, the message to the political actor is likely to be, 'If you want to get to Dublin, I wouldn't start from here.' Illuminating perhaps, but massively unhelpful. The states of Eastern Europe in the years after 1989 were not short of academic advice and academic advisers. None of this activity seems to have had any systematically helpful influence on their subsequent developments.

The elaboration of theories versus the clarification of language

There is a danger that political science will become a battle of abstract concepts, models, theories which fight for the right to impose their rule on reality. But since any theory is an abbreviation of evidence, any model a simplification of what can be observed, the greater the dominance of any particular theory, the greater the alienation from historical or empirical reality. The artificiality of much discussion of this type is evident in arguments about which theory is correct, or whether identity can be seen to shape legitimacy, or legitimacy qualify identity.

My intention is more cautious and less ambitious: an account of possible ingredients of political situations, without hoping to be able to be even so certain as that about their likely or possible combinations or outcomes. The warnings of Hirschman after the events of 1989 in Eastern Europe are thoroughly apposite here: 'It does not seem to have occurred to these people that if the events, which are the points of departure of their speculations, were so hard to predict, considerable caution is surely in order when it comes to appraising their impact.'[23] Whilst I have drawn on both theory and empirical and historical research in the following chapters, I have adopted an eclectic stance, which views theoretical discussion as an attempt to clarify language, which then can be used in a flexible, non-dogmatic, and multidimensional way in the examination of political life.

---

[23] Albert O. Hirschman, 'Good News is Not Bad News', *New York Review of Books*, 11 October 1990, 20, quoted Guiseppe Di Palma, 'Legitimation from the Top to Civil Society: Politico-Cultural Change in Eastern Europe', *World Politics* 44, 1 (October 1991), p. 79.

CHAPTER 3

King John's Christmas cards: self-legitimation

King John was not a good man,
And no good friends had he.
He stayed in every afternoon . . .
But no one came to tea.
And, round about December,
The cards upon his shelf
Which wished him lots of Christmas cheer,
And fortune in the coming year,
Were never from his near and dear,
But only from himself.[1]

A. A. Milne's King John provides a metaphor, if an exaggerated one, for the self-legitimation of government. In addition to the picture of legitimation frequently presented, as the means whereby subjects and, ideally, subjects in a democracy, authorise government, or rulers gain the consent of the ruled, legitimation is also an activity carried on by rulers for their own benefit, by the state for and from itself. Legitimation is not only a circus for the mass of subjects, but also a private theatre for rulers, where they see their own identity portrayed, confirmed, and justified. The near and dear, inasmuch as they are part of the community of rulers, will send cards, but nobody else will. The larger part of the population will not even know that the ceremonies are occurring. Rulers appear to need to legitimate their power, to demonstrate constantly by rituals both spiritual and secular their unique prestige, as persons authorised in a manner that ordinary subjects are not, as persons set apart to exercise the powers and privileges of government. This attribution of apparent need rests neither on a deductive view of what

[1] A. A. Milne, *Now We Are Six* (London, Methuen, 1927, 1989 edn) p. 2.

rulers require, nor on an empirical psychology of rulers. Rather, as with Weber, it is a matter of observing the regularity with which rulers, of all kinds and in all kinds of regimes, engage in legitimation. The attribution of need is therefore a hypothetical explanation of observed behaviour, not a theory about governmental behaviour with predictive aspirations. It depends upon the assumption that if a group of people consistently behave in a certain way, that behaviour can reasonably be described as arising from need rather than whim or contingency. It could, alternatively, be seen as a constitutive need in the same way that animals need warm blood in order to be mammals – without it they would not be mammals, and the need is a need for certain characteristics or functions in order to be one thing rather than another.

THREE GROUPS OF ACTORS

In the drama of legitimation there are three groups: custodians – rulers, kings, presidents, prime ministers – all those engaged in governing; cousins, the 'near and dear' – those who stand in a privileged position in relation to the custodians without themselves actually governing; and subjects – the ordinary citizens, voters, and people. Different identities are formed and operate within the world of custodians, within the world of cousins, and within the world of citizens. The world of cousins forms a mediating one between custodians and citizens, influencing both and drawing on the strengths of both. But a drama is acted out by the custodians, in which ordinary citizens and subjects play no part, and where the plot is constructed within a structure composed of the needs, satisfactions and conventions of the private world of government.

DEMOCRATIC AND MOST POST-WEBER THEORY ASSUMES THAT LEGITIMATION IS ENGAGED IN BY CUSTODIANS AS AN INSTRUMENT OF RULE

This attention to the world of rulers stands at some remove from most recent political science. The prevailing use of the terms legitimation and legitimacy is to indicate the conferring of authority on government by citizens, or the acceptance by citizens of the right of government to rule because the appropriate criteria of efficiency, or fairness, or probity, or representativeness have been met. The activity described is of government as the recipient or beneficiary of acts or beliefs of subjects, rather than an active and initiating agent. And in so far as government does act, its actions are seen not as part of the business of legitimation, but as the evidence upon which the court of public opinion will make its judgement about the acceptability of the regime. Legitimation is the school report which the electorate issues on the governmental term rather than one of the distinguishing features of government itself.[2] When legitimation is seen to be a problem, it is a problem because government has failed to fulfil the expectations of citizens, whether in the case of conventional states,[3] or in the case of international institutions of governance such as the European Union.[4]

There is both a theoretical and a methodological or practical reason for the direction of attention away from the self-legitimation of government. Political science, for much of the twentieth century, and since the reaction against the elitism of the late nineteenth and early twentieth centuries, has been a democratic discipline. Normatively government has been justified by its representation of the views, and protection and promotion of the interests, of citizens. To give an account of normative activity within government which seemed to owe little directly to public consent could seem to confer approval on elites and to free them from the qualifying test of public approval or consent.[5] For the purposes of research, it has been far easier to study the actions and opinions of citizens

[2] T. R. Gurr, *Why Men Rebel* (Princeton, Princeton University Press, 1970), p. 186; Rodney Barker, *Political Legitimacy and the State* (Oxford, Clarendon, 1990), pp. 66–83, 107–28; and chapter 6 below.
[3] '"*legitimacy*" is just a suspension of withdrawal of consent' and it 'will no longer be granted if it does not find real corollaries in material interests', Adam Przeworski, *Capitalism and Social Democracy* (Cambridge, Cambridge University Press, 1985), p. 146.
[4] See, for instance, Simon Hix, 'The Study of the European Union II: the "new governance" agenda and its rival', *Journal of European Public Policy* 5, 1 (1998), 38–65.
[5] This objection is raised specifically in the case of the analysis of the state by Geoffrey Marshall who argues that the concept of a coherent state has consequences for the potential of such an institution to flourish, and the ability of republicans to resist it: 'for Republicans the struggle to subject the executive to law begins with a conceptual struggle to separate and clarify what the term "State" confuses', Geoffrey Marshall, *Constitutional Theory* (Oxford, Oxford University Press, 1971), p. 34.

than the internal behaviour of government. The closer the centre of power is approached, the more practice, convention, etiquette, ideology and law narrow and impede the view. When government has been seen therefore as itself engaged in legitimation, this activity has been perceived predominantly or exclusively, as it was by Marx, as part of the ruling strategy of manipulating the people.[6] The 'rites of rulers',[7] as analysed by Robert Goodin, are the circuses which government adds to the bread of welfare in order to cultivate popular support. Goodin's examination of these rites or rituals significantly slips from referring to them as rituals of rulers to calling them political rituals, rituals which serve, in other words, a persuasive function in the world of citizens and subjects. But the rituals of rulers are also governmental rituals and may, like the more esoteric religious rituals, be carried out away from the public gaze. Goodin's discussion of the medieval European priesthood draws attention to the way in which the withdrawal of the priest beyond the rood screen to celebrate mass was a ritual expression of the subordinate position of the peasantry, who were visibly excluded from the ceremony.[8] But were that all that was happening, and were this simply or solely a means of expressing and reinforcing the subordination of the laity, once the priest was removed from the sight of the congregation he would need to do no more, but wait for a time before reappearing. In fact, of course he did a very great deal more, and the witness to the ceremony, if others were there at all, was provided by other members of the priesthood and immediate servants of the altar. The 'secret' ceremony was only secret if one assumes that it was solely for public consumption. As Peter Berger long ago pointed out, for legitimation to work, it has to be more than a device to fool the masses. The practitioners have to believe just as much as everyone else does; the 'children must be convinced, but so must be their teachers'.[9]

---

[6] Barker, *Political Legitimacy and the State*, pp. 85–6.

[7] Robert E. Goodin, 'Rites of Rulers' in Goodin, *Manipulatory Politics* (New Haven and London, Yale University Press, 1980).

[8] Ibid., p. 179.

[9] Peter L. Berger, *The Sacred Canopy: Elements of a Sociological Theory of Religion* (Garden City, NY, Doubleday, 1967), p. 31. This is the opposite of the view taken by Jeremy Rayner, who argues that in order to succeed, the leaders of belief have to encourage views which they do not themselves hold: Jeremy Rayner, 'Philosophy into Dogma: The Revival of Cultural Conservatism', *British Journal of Political Science* 16, 4 (October 1986), 455–74.

LEGITIMATION OF RULERS, BY RULERS, FOR RULERS

What has frequently been ignored is that, as Weber pointed out, legitimacy functions as self-justification for the administrative personnel of government. It may well be, though he did not argue this, that this is the most important function and location of legitimation.[10] No party, faction, class or group, Weber suggested, is ever content to control simply the coercive and administrative means of government. There is in fact some ambiguity in Weber's own account here. One part of his argument certainly suggests that legitimation is carried on because 'custom, personal advantage, purely affectual or ideal motives of solidarity, do not form a sufficiently reliable basis for a given domination'.[11] This utilitarian function exists because 'the basis of every authority, and correspondingly of every kind of willingness to obey, is a *belief*, a belief by virtue of which persons exercising authority are lent prestige'.[12] But two aspects of the argument are often neglected. First, that Weber is here describing the relations between 'the chief and his administrative staff',[13] not those between rulers and ruled. Second, that he elsewhere suggests that the activity of legitimation, whatever its function in sustaining the solidarity of immediate subordinates, also functions to sustain the ruler himself: 'he who is more favoured feels the never ceasing need to look upon his position as in some way "legitimate"'.[14] Some commentators have elided these various points, so that even the passage quoted above is presented as an account of a purely instrumental function whereby rulers

[10] Beetham and Lord suggest that 'Analysts of political legitimacy from Max Weber onwards have argued about whether the recognition or acknowledgement of a regime's legitimacy is only important to the behaviour of its elites or administrative staff, rather than of subjects more widely', David Beetham and Christopher Lord, *Legitimacy and the European Union* (London, Longman, 1998), p. 10. But they do not develop the point, nor do they sustain it with citation or discussion of work which has paid attention to legitimation within elites. Beetham's and Lord's use of the words 'recognition or acknowledgement' is interesting. The main focus of their argument, as of Beetham's own earlier argument, is that legitimacy is an objective status earned by regimes, and earned principally though not exclusively through their fulfilment of democratic criteria of representativeness and procedure. To speak of 'recognition or acknowledgement' is not inconsistent with this, but it does focus on the regime, rather than on the procedures, context, or history which in Beetham's and Lord's terms, justifies it.
[11] Max Weber, *Economy and Society*, Guenther Roth and Claus Wittich (eds.), 2 vols. (London, University of California Press, 1978), vol. I, p. 213.
[12] Ibid., p. 263.   [13] Ibid., p. 213.   [14] Ibid., p. 953.

sustain the obedience of the mass of their subjects. Joseph Berger and Morris Zelditch write that

The supposedly most powerful actor in society is, in fact, dependent on the subordinates who actually control the facilities of force. Their loyalty might be bought with side payments, and the larger population bought with promises of benefits, but inducements are also unstable in the long run. The value of inducements depends on the preferences of the subordinates, which vary over actors and across time. Hence, every system of domination attempts to cultivate a belief in its legitimacy.

Weber's point is glossed by the incorporation of his words into Berger's and Zelditch's own text, but with the addition of the word 'hence'.[15] But the seemingly ubiquitous priority given to this activity, the activity of legitimation, deserves attention. Equal attention, and by way of compensation for relative neglect even greater attention, needs to be given to one other vital feature of Weber's original comments. Weber wrote of 'the claims of obedience made by the master against the "officials" and of both against the ruled'.[16] Legitimation is an activity, in other words, carried on within government. And not only is legitimation carried out by government, it is frequently carried out for government, and for the private satisfaction of government rather than for its public acclaim. There is an observable and universal need to justify the possession of government by claiming legitimacy. 'The fortunate is seldom satisfied with the fact of being fortunate. Beyond this, he needs to know that he has a *right* to his good fortune . . . Good fortune thus wants to be "legitimate" fortune.'[17] 'Simple observation shows that in every such situation he who is more favored feels the never ceasing need to look upon his position as in some way "legitimate", upon his advantage as "deserved", and the other's disadvantage as being brought about by the latter's "fault".'[18] Drawing on Weber amongst others, Dolf Sternberg appeared to have no doubts on the matter. 'Legitimacy is the foundation of such governmental power as is

[15] Joseph Berger and Morris Zelditch, *Status, Power and Legitimacy* (London, Transaction Books, 1996), p. 267.
[16] Weber, *Economy and Society*, p. 953.
[17] Weber in H. H. Gerth and C. W. Mills (eds.), *From Max Weber: Essays in Sociology* (London, 1948), p. 271.
[18] Weber, *Economy and Society*, p. 953.

exercised both with a consciousness on the government's part that it has a right to govern and with some recognition by the governed of that right.'[19] The word 'some' is of greater significance than the ranking of the parties. Applying this observation to the rulers of imperial Rome, Paul Veyne comments that this 'tendency of the sovereign's to express his majesty is no more rational than his need to justify himself: the means are not proportionate to the ends. Justification and expression lend themselves secondarily to ideological use or to "machiavellian" rationalisations, but they are not primarily weapons' . . . 'the king wants to satisfy himself and has little notion of the effects his ostentation produces on the spectator'.[20] As David Kertzer comments, 'In order to invest a person with authority over others, there must be an effective means for changing the way other people view that person, as well as for changing the person's conception of his right to impose his will on others.'[21] His own conception of himself appears to be an essential element in the business. Veyne's comparison of non-rational legitimation with '"machiavellian" rationalisations' is illuminatingly inappropriate. Machiavelli's own account of the aims of rulers places just such apparently non-rational or non-utilitarian goals to the fore. Rulers seek not wealth or material comfort, but prestige, greatness, and honour.[22] Some of the actions of rulers can be explained in terms of the desire for tangible goods. But that does not give a sufficient explanation. And whilst it may provide important clues to marginal changes – which may be of great significance in their consequences – it cannot explain the choice of rule, as against the choice of banking or ballet. The analysis of power must share dissatisfactions with mere or narrow utilitarianism which are analogous to those felt by John Stuart Mill.

The need for self-justification amongst rulers seems universal. When Henry III spent the equivalent of two entire years' royal income on creating Westminster Abbey as a declaration of both the

[19] Dolf Sternberg, 'Legitimacy' in *The International Encyclopaedia of the Social Sciences*, vol. IX, pp. 244–8 (New York, 1968), p. 244.
[20] Paul Veyne, *Bread and Circuses: Historical Sociology and Political Pluralism*, trans. Brian Pearce (London, Penguin, 1992), p. 380.
[21] David L. Kertzer, *Ritual, Politics, and Power* (New Haven and London, Yale University Press, 1988), p. 24.
[22] Niccolò Machiavelli, *The Prince* ([1532] Cambridge, Cambridge University Press, 1988).

sanctity of Edward the Confessor and the legitimation by association of his own kingship,[23] the likely audience was a tiny fragment
of the population. As Paul Binski comments on the architectural
and iconographic demonstration of royal legitimation which the
abbey constituted, the manifestation was 'not to some notional
"public", but rather to the community which produced it in the
first place'.[24] And the most important receiver of the sacramen-
tal royal message was perhaps the king himself. Even when such
religious construction or ritual was publicly displayed, as when
Henry V spent almost as much on the reburial of Richard II as
he had spent on the funeral of his own father who had usurped
Richard,[25] the public was limited, and the most privileged observer was Henry himself. As Paul Strohm comments, 'Well might
a Lancastrian, besieged by apparitions and rumors, hope to close
the troubled space of their origin by returning Richard to his proper
grave. Henry V's decision to effect this return is here treated not as
an isolated act of piety but as a positive political stratagem – a form
of symbolic struggle which addressed (though it could not settle)
continuing problems of Lancastrian legitimation.'[26] But problems
for whom? Such endogenous, regnal self-legitimation is not an activity peculiar to either monarchy or the European middle ages.
At the end of the twentieth century, the Iraqi President Sadam
Hussein possessed many presidential palaces. But the only occasion on which they were entered by the people of Iraq was during 1998 when those ordinary subjects were brought in to deter
American and British air raids. Presidential palaces are to impress
presidents, not subjects. Nor is the seclusion of palaces and their
reservation for the ruler and his immediate entourage a feature
peculiar to despotic or undemocratic regimes. The degree of seclusion will differ markedly, but even the rulers of the most politically egalitarian regimes will have their distinctiveness marked by
the buildings which they use. Harold Lasswell and Merritt Fox
contrast autocratic separation, the Forbidden City or the Kremlin

[23] Paul Binski, *Westminster Abbey and the Plantagenets* (New Haven, Yale University Press, 1995),
     p. 1.
[24] Ibid., p. 9.
[25] Paul Strohm, *England's Empty Throne: Usurpation and the Language of Legitimation, 1399–1422*
     (London, Yale University Press, 1998), pp. 115–16.
[26] Ibid., p. 103.

under both tzars and communism, with popular government in the United States:

The sharpest contrast to despotism and autocracy is a well-established popular government. The official meets the citizen on a common level and the chief of state lives with an insignificant physical barrier separating him from his fellows. The White House in Washington expresses the basic relationship that connects the transitory holder of the presidential office and the rank and file of the nation. The White House is neither remote nor exalted; it has the approachability of a private home.[27]

But the White House is clearly far more 'exalted' than the average American home, and significantly less approachable. The citizens of the United States may visit and be impressed by the White House once or even several times in a lifetime,[28] but the president can be impressed by it, and what it says about the incumbent of the presidential office, every day. According to Edelman,'That a man meets with his aides in the Oval Office of the White House reminds him and them and the public to whom the meeting is reported of his status and authority as President, just as it exalts the status of the aides and defines the mass public as nonparticipants who never enter the Office.'[29]

There is a substantial literature in political psychology on the internal or personal satisfactions of power, which I have not touched upon, and whose concerns, though relevant to the wider discussion of power and legitimation, lie on the borders of what I deal with here.[30] Harold Lasswell saw leadership as arising from the need to work out private problems in public places, Erik Erikson considered leadership as a conjunction of personal history and social situation.[31] But it is possible to speculate about the nature of any

[27] Harold D. Lasswell and Merritt B. Fox, *The Signature of Power: Buildings, Communication, and Policy* (New Brunswick, NJ, Transaction Books, 1979), p. 16.
[28] They can now visit a virtual White House whenever they wish, and tour its public spaces. www.whitehouse.gov/. Circuses have been replaced by vdus.
[29] Murray Edelman, 'Space and the Social Order', *Journal of Architectural Education* 32, 3 (November 1978), 2 7, p. 2.
[30] See, for instance, Robert E. Lane, 'Experiencing Money and Experiencing Power', in Ian Shapiro and Grant Reeher (eds.), *Power, Inequality, and Democratic Politics: Essays in Honour of Robert A. Dahl* (Boulder and London, Westview Press, 1988); David C. McClelland, *Power: the Inner Experience* (New York, Irvington Publishers, 1975).
[31] Dankwart A. Rustow (ed.), *Philosophers and Kings: Studies in Leadership* (New York, George Braziller, 1970).

'need' for self-legitimating identity cultivation without crossing into psychology. Rulers can be depicted as seeking ethical or perceptual coherence, a fit between their account of themselves, and their other actions. This search for coherence, whilst it might be investigated in terms of its psychological dimension, can be described also as a feature of the actions of rulers. Inis Claude remarks illuminatingly that 'power holders are burdened, like other human beings, by the necessity of satisfying their own consciences. By and large, they cannot comfortably regard themselves as usurpers or tyrants but require some basis for convincing themselves of the rightness of their position.'[32] It can be suggested that such legitimation serves to consolidate ruling groups,[33] providing the self-justification that enables elites to function, not with the consent of their subjects, but with the consent of their own conception of themselves and their social and governmental identities.

The effort devoted to legitimation within the community of governors is a feature of the effort to cultivate an appropriate identity. Because the identity of rulers is of greatest importance to rulers themselves, the cultivation of governing identity, the legitimation of rule, becomes more important the further up the governmental tree one climbs. Legitimation is the legitimation of an activity by describing, cultivating, and identifying it and its actor in a particular way: the more that people engage in the activity, the more legitimation they are likely to engage in. This account of legitimation and its location is consonant with Weber's conception of elective affinity: the legitimating ideas and concepts are adopted, refined, and cultivated with a vigour relative to the extent to which the person or group is engaged in the activity of governing, and has therefore the interests which go with that occupation. But one can also observe that the more demanding the activity, the more

---

[32] Inis L. Claude, Jr, 'Collective Legitimization as a Political Function of the United Nations', *International Organization* 20 (1966), 367–79, p. 368.

[33] Ibid.: 'How was system integration sustained in imperial societies? Three sets of factors seem most important: the use of coercive sanctions, based on military power; the legitimation of authority *within ruling elites*, making possible the establishment of an administrative apparatus of government; and the formation of economic ties of interdependence'; Anthony Giddens, *A Contemporary Critique of Historical Materialism* (London, Macmillan, 1981), p. 103: 'This is not to say that the legitimation of power was unimportant in the system integration of imperial societies; but its significance is to be found primarily in terms of how far it helped to consolidate the ruling apparatus itself.'

necessary the legitimation. And governing is a far more time-consuming (though not necessarily more onerous) activity than being governed. Amongst the various forms of political legitimation, the legitimation carried out by rulers is the most important – and it is accorded by them to themselves.

This endogenous regnal self-legitimation of rulers in their own eyes and for their own consumption is a major feature of government, and a minor feature of politics. It is, in an amendment of the Gettysburg phrases, legitimation of government, by government, and for government. To ignore this is to ignore a major feature of all government. The proper and desirable wish of political scientists to establish normative criteria for assessing government, to do so in conjunction with the procedures of democracy, and hence to present legitimation as a public communication between rulers and ruled has been accompanied by a neglect of another world of legitimation. This diversion of attention is sustained, or not challenged, by the behaviour of government itself. The way in which government sets about legitimating itself contributes to this lacuna in political science, since legitimation, however much it may have a public face, is in the first place carried on relatively privately. It is in the first place for the benefit of rulers, not of subjects, and is pursued in the sight of rulers, not in the sight of the ruled. It can be argued that legitimation is necessary to subjects not to cause them to obey, but to enable them to obey. But it may be equally necessary to enable rulers to issue commands by confirming them in their belief that they have the authority to do so, that they act in a way which confirms and cultivates their particular legitimating identity as rulers.

LEGITIMATION OF RULERS IN THEIR OWN EYES

For the legitimation which is carried out, initiated, and directed by rulers, the rulers themselves are the principal audience. Even when recognition is cultivated in others, it is most actively sought from the rulers' own immediate associates, institution, or community. The principal focus of the activity of legitimation is the rulers themselves. It is for their own self-definition, rather than for their justification in the eyes of their subjects, that legitimation is principally

conducted. A royal marriage may be, as Bagehot put it, the brilliant
edition of a universal fact,[34] but rulers may seek a confirmation of
this distinctiveness out of the public gaze as well as in it. It is not only
Pharisees who thank God that they are not as other men.[35] Peter
Burke, in his account of the legitimation of Louis XIV, comments
that one of the audiences was posterity.[36] It could be argued in development of this point that a concern for posterity is a concern for
one's own survival, an attempt to reassure oneself that mortality can
be transcended. Certainly, impressing posterity does not contribute
to the grip on power of the living. As Burke elsewhere observes, the
effects of legitimation need to be considered, 'not least on the king
himself'[37] who, after all, amidst the wealth of iconography, 'saw
himself everywhere, even on the ceiling'.[38] The function of ceremony in confirming the sense of the principal actor of his or her
authority can be detected as readily in twentieth-century France as
under the monarchy of the seventeenth and eighteenth centuries.
François Mitterand consulted experts on the rituals and symbols
of the revolution of 1789 when planning his own presidential in-
auguration in 1981.[39] However many or few might appreciate the
significance of the resulting ceremonial detail, the new president
would do so. The difference was in this respect not great between a
president, and a king for whom the 'panegyrics in prose and verse
were addressed in the first place to an audience of one, the king
himself'.[40] Paul Veyne comments of the justificatory displays of
imperial Rome that the ruler 'is ready to proclaim his own glory
even if nobody is listening'.[41] Sometimes even the presidents and
princes may have difficulty gaining effective sight or experience of
the artefacts of legitimation. But they know they are there, whereas

[34] Quoted in David Cannadine, 'Introduction: Divine Rites of Kings' in David Cannadine
and Simon Price (eds.), *Rituals of Royalty: Power and Ceremonial in Traditional Societies*
(Cambridge, Cambridge University Press, 1987), p. 16.
[35] Luke 18, 11.
[36] Peter Burke, *The Fabrication of Louis XIV* (New Haven, Yale University Press, 1992), p. 153.
[37] Ibid., p. 7.
[38] Ibid., p. 17.
[39] Sean Wilentz, 'Introduction: Teufelsdröckh's Dilemma: On Symbolism, Politics, and
History' in Sean Wilentz (ed.), *Rites of Power: Symbolism, Ritual and Politics Since the Middle
Ages* (Philadelphia, University of Pennsylvania Press, 1985), p. 5.
[40] Burke, *The Fabrication of Louis XIV*, p. 152.
[41] Veyne, *Bread and Circuses*, p. 380.

for the population as a whole they may be, by their location or their very character, inaccessible. Veyne writes of the effectively invisible frieze celebrating, on Trajan's column, the emperor's military triumphs in Dacia, 'Archaeologists examine this frieze with binoculars. We may doubt whether Trajan's subjects paid much more attention to it.'[42]

One of the ways in which rulers legitimate themselves is by the construction or development of physical environments which express and confirm their governing identity. Leaders surround themselves with objects which 'acknowledge' their importance. Louis XIV was frequently portrayed in the midst of 'a whole cluster of dignified or dignity-bestowing properties such as orbs, sceptres, swords, thunderbolts, chariots and various kinds of military trophy'.[43] The juxtaposition of people with objects 'proclaims' authority. It might seem that such activity is invalid unless carried out in the public gaze, and that privacy negates the exercise. The reverse is the case. It follows from the logic of such legitimation that other people should not be in juxtaposition with the legitimating objects, or at least not at the same time as the leader. It is the objects which announce authority, and if the leaders shared that juxtaposition with others, the announcement would either be shared with them, or be evaporated and meaningless. The very bath water of the West African kings of Akuapem is specially disposed of, to prevent mere ordinary humans using it and hence acquiring something of the distinctiveness of royalty.[44] Only if the leaders can be seen in exclusive proximity to the authority acknowledging objects can the magic still work. So when kings of Akuapem were enthroned, or enstooled, the ritual took place beyond the public view. The articulation and enactment of their special character was conducted in private.[45] English kings and queens, though crowned before witnesses, were similarly anointed in the view of God alone.

What is the peculiar contribution of objects and the manufactured world to legitimation? Cannot people, subjects, acknowledge

[42] Ibid., p. 381.
[43] Burke, *The Fabrication of Louis XIV*, p. 33.
[44] Michelle Gilbert, 'The Person of the King: Ritual and Power in a Ghanaian State' in Cannadine and Price (eds.), *Rituals of Royalty*, p. 328.
[45] Ibid.

authority? They can, but they are neither so malleable nor so reliable as objects, nor so permanently on call. The Wilton Diptych, the devotional painting which formed part of the portable possessions of Richard II, 'served to focus Richard's own meditation, to re-enact his devotion, whether he was present or not, to proclaim to himself the certainty of his prospective welcome in Heaven, and finally, to reinforce his idea of earthly kingship under heavenly protection'.[46] The diptych was for private, not public display, but was an assertion for the king of his authority and his unique status in relation to God and man. Paul Binski comments on Richard's devotion to the royal shrine which Westminster Abbey had become, that it reflected 'the peculiar anxieties of an insecure, fastidious and hypersensitive young king'.[47] The assuaging of royal anxieties was for the king alone. It was his doubts that were calmed, his sense of authority that was confirmed. His consciousness, not that of his subjects, was the focus. The rituals of power, from Versailles to Nuremberg, from Delhi to Washington, however much they may impress the subjects and citizens of their regimes, impress the rulers at least as much. A triumphal entry into Rome may have been accompanied by a whispered reminder, 'Remember you are mortal',[48] but the triumphal quotidian life of rulers is accompanied by the far louder statement, 'Remember you are not like others.'[49]

The secret garden of government

The public, though they may be an audience, have never been the principal audience in the theatre of endogenous legitimation, of the 'courtly rituals which are unknown to or unobserved by the majority of the population'[50] and which coexist with public displays. The

---

[46] Lucy Freeman Sandler, 'The Wilton Diptych and Images of Devotion in Illuminated Manuscripts' in Gillian Gordon, Lisa Monnas, and Caroline Elam (eds.), *The Regal Image of Richard II and the Wilton Diptych* (London, Harvey Miller Publishers, 1998), p. 154.

[47] Binski, *Westminster Abbey and the Plantagenets*, p. 200.

[48] Ernst H. Kantorowicz, *The King's Two Bodies* (Princeton, Princeton University Press, 1957), p. 496.

[49] Ibid., Kantorowicz quotes Francis Bacon on this point, to the effect that the two precepts '*Memento quod es homo*' and '*Memento quod es deus, or vice Dei*' between them check the power and the will of kings, p. 496. But the checks imposed by the first are balanced by the power which comes from the authorising identification of oneself as unique.

[50] Cannadine, 'Introduction: Divine Rites of Kings', p. 13.

'theatre state' of Bali described by Clifford Geertz, with its massive emphasis on spectacle and ceremony, where 'Power served pomp, not pomp power',[51] was not an exotic oddity, but simply an extravagant point on a single continuum.[52] Sydney Anglo comments on the arrival of Henry VII in London after the Battle of Bosworth, that it was 'for the great majority of ordinary folk who made up the cheering roadside throng on the way to the capital, probably the last time that they ever saw their monarch in the flesh'.[53] Hence 'One of the greatest obstacles barring the way to a sensible appreciation of the ways in which Renaissance rulers were perceived by their contemporaries is that we know a great deal more about these kings and queens than did even the best informed of their subjects. It is true that we cannot hear their voices, interview them or see them in the flesh: but in these respects we are no worse off than all but their tiny circle of intimates.'[54] This was not an accidental or random effect. Government is a secret garden, and its ceremonies, rituals, and life both exceptional and mundane serve to mark off even its most egalitarian practitioners from those whom they rule. The message is an externally directed one but, even more importantly, an internally directed one, confirming the legitimating identity of the ruling group. Terence Ranger and Olufemi Vaughan comment that the 'need for rulers to be confident in their own legitimacy and to define their relations with other members of the ruling group underlies those "secret" rituals of kingship of which the general population of African states often seem to be ignorant'.[55] The

---

[51] Clifford Geertz, *Negara: The Theatre State in Nineteenth Century Bali* (Princeton, Princeton University Press, 1980), p. 13. Though Gordon Kipling has drawn on Geertz's conceptions to draw conclusions with a different emphasis for medieval Europe: 'The pageants may, indeed, "flatter and cajole" the prince, but their primary purpose lay in celebrating and renewing the communal political bond which united the sovereign and his people', Gordon Kipling, *Enter the King: Theatre, Liturgy and Ritual in the Medieval Civic Triumph* (Oxford, Oxford University Press, 1986), p. 47.

[52] It is one, too, which received fictional depiction over a quarter of a century before Geertz employed it as a means of anthropological explanation. The world described by Mervyn Peak in his first two Gormenghast novels is precisely driven by the need to continue and enact ceremony. Mervyn Peake, *Titus Groan* (London, Eyre and Spotiswood, 1946); *Gormenghast* (London, Eyre and Spotiswood, 1950).

[53] Sydney Anglo, *Images of Tudor Kingship* (London, B.A. Seaby, 1992), p. 98.

[54] Ibid., p. 1.

[55] Terence Ranger and Olufemi Vaughan, 'Introduction' in Terence Ranger and Olufemi Vaughan (eds.), *Legitimacy and the State in Twentieth-Century Africa: Essays in Honour of A. H. M. Kirk-Greene* (London, Macmillan, 1993), p. 8.

message of ritual and ceremony can be disseminated not just by
formal, institutional distinctions, but by the entire culture of rule.
As Benedict Anderson observes of pre-colonial Java, 'Although the
ruling class of traditional Java could be defined in structural terms
as the hierarchy of officials and their extended families, like any
other ruling class they were also marked off – indeed marked themselves off – from the rest of the population by their style of life and
self-consciously espoused system of values.'[56] The use of expert
languages, for instance, whether Mandarin or managerial strategic
military jargon, serves both to exclude the bulk of the population
from the exchange, and to indicate to the users of the language
their special status, their particular identity and justification. The
elaborate ritual codes of the T'ang dynasty in China were the key to
ceremonial events which, though they might on occasion have public spectators, were in the first place the preserve of a ruling elite.[57]
In a society as apparently open and public as nineteenth-century
Britain, its royal rituals could still have an essentially private character: 'great royal ceremonials were not so much shared, corporate
events as remote, inaccessible group rites, performed for the benefit
of the few rather than the edification of the many'.[58] Even when the
legitimating message is ostensibly public, the manner of its trans-
mission, and the limited nature of the public, can make it an almost
private communication. The audience of 'privy councillors, court
hangers-on, continental observers, university scholars, and British
clerics' described by Lori Ferrell for the sermons emanating from
the court of James I & VI was quite select.[59] Even funerals could be
occasions for such enactments, as Jennifer Woodward comments

[56] Benedict R. O'G. Anderson, 'The Idea of Power in Javanese Culture' in Claire Holt (ed.),
with the assistance of Benedict R. O'G. Anderson and James Siegel, *Culture and Politics in
Indonesia*, 1–69 (Ithaca, Cornell University Press, 1972), p. 38.

[57] David McMullen, 'Bureaucrats and Cosmology: The Ritual Code of T'ang China' in
Cannadine and Price (eds.), *Rituals of Royalty*.

[58] David Cannadine, 'The Context, Performance and Meaning of Ritual: The British
Monarchy and the "Invention of Tradition", *c.* 1820–1977' in Eric Hobsbawm and
Terence Ranger (eds.), *The Invention of Tradition*, pp. 101–64 (Cambridge, Cambridge
University Press, 1983), p. 111. Interestingly, the illustration on the cover of the paperback edition of *The Invention of Tradition* shows just such an 'inaccessible group rite', the
presentation of a dead stag by Albert to Victoria and her children, by flaming torch light,
at a door to Balmoral.

[59] Lori Anne Ferrell, *Government by Polemic: James I, the King's Preachers, and the Rhetorics of
Conformity, 1603–1625* (Stanford, Stanford University Press, 1998), p. 11.

of the royal obsequies of Renaissance England: 'By taking part
in the procession each individual acknowledged and enacted his
relative status in society.'[60] Pierre Bourdieu, discussing the educa-
tional recruitment, and selection, of the twentieth-century French
elite, argues that ceremonies and procedures of initiation transform
'the representation that the invested person has of himself, and the
behaviour he feels obliged to adopt in order to conform to that
representation'.[61] But it is not only in the entry into an elite, but
in the entire subsequent life of its members, that their identity is
legitimated, and their identification legitimates their position.

Writing of the Soviet Union before 1989, Joseph Schull comments on the importance of ideology not as a means of commu-
nicating with or persuading the mass of the population, but as a
means of legitimating governing elites in their own eyes:

> The masses were simply not the audience to whom political claims were
> legitimated. In these societies, ideology was essentially the language of
> political elites who constrained *each other* to obey its conventions. When the
> leaders of these societies used ideology to legitimate some claim, they were
> speaking to their colleagues as the co-tenants of ideological orthodoxy, not
> to the population at large. This is not to say that Marxism-Leninism was
> not propagated to the masses in such societies. Of course it was, but this
> was not the arena in which *ideological discourse* (as opposed to propaganda)
> was taking place.[62]

Schull could equally well have been writing of Louis XIV, of
whose copiously produced iconography Peter Burke commented
that it was 'unlikely that it was intended for the mass of Louis'
subjects'.[63] As Norbert Elias commented on the court of Louis,
and on courts in general, 'The practice of etiquette is, in other
words, an exhibition of court society to itself. Each participant,
above all the king, has his prestige and his relative power position confirmed by others... The immense value attached to the
demonstration of prestige and the observance of etiquette does not

---

[60] Jennifer Woodward, *The Theatre of Death: The Ritual Management of Royal Funerals in Renaissance England, 1570–1625* (Woodbridge, Boydell Press, 1997), p. 24.

[61] Pierre Bourdieu, *Language and Symbolic Power*, ed. John B. Thompson, trans. Gino Raymond and Matthew Adamson (Cambridge, Polity, 1991), p. 119.

[62] Joseph Schull, 'What is Ideology? Theoretical Problems and Lessons from Soviet-Type
Societies', *Political Studies* 40, 4 (December 1992), 728–41, p. 737.

[63] Burke, *The Fabrication of Louis XIV*, p. 151.

betray an attachment to externals, but to what was vitally important to individual identity.'[64] Many of the rituals of kingship and
its creation have been in this way, as David Cannadine remarks,
'unknown to or unobserved by the majority of the population'.[65]

Architecture can be a powerful expression of such political facts
and political aspirations. The character of capital cities, the style of
their buildings and the construction of the spaces which link them,
can forcefully express the claims of government. Chandigarh, the
state capital of the Indian Punjab, despite being part of a formal
democracy, said more about the independent authority of rulers
than about the rights or participation of citizens, with 'pedestrian
resistant' expanses of plaza.[66] Brasília, similarly, was constructed
in a way which 'effectively discouraged mass involvement'.[67] As
Murray Edelman put it, 'Settings not only condition political acts.
They mold the very personalities of the actors.'[68] Space, and the
guarding and marking of space, pronounced to those who could
enter or occupy the forbidden cities of government that they were
marked off from ordinary people. The very difficulty and compli-
cation of reaching the king, or the president, or the prime minister,
the layers of courts and courtiers through which it was necessary to
pass, proclaimed to those who were in the inner sanctum or who
were given access to it, how exceptional they were.

LEADERS AND IMMEDIATE FOLLOWERS

The persons exercising governing power can be variously
described: as ruler or rulers, as governing elite, as the entire personnel of the state. A frequent and useful distinction is that between the
relatively small number of people who either directly or indirectly
command the system of government, and the mass of the population. Weber, for instance, speaks of 'the chief and his administrative

---

[64] Norbert Elias, *The Court Society*, trans. Edmund Jephcott (Oxford, Blackwell, 1983), p. 101.

[65] Cannadine, 'Introduction: Divine Rites of Kings', p. 13.

[66] Lawrence J. Vale, *Architecture, Power and National Identity* (New Haven: Yale University Press, 1992), p. 113.

[67] Ibid., p. 127.

[68] Murray Edelman, *The Symbolic Uses of Politics* (London, University of Illinois Press, 1964), p. 108; 'We should expect, then, that a person's values, style of life and of political action, and expectation of others' roles would be shaped by his social setting, symbolic and nonsymbolic', p. 109.

King John's Christmas 59

staff', and contrasts them with 'subjects', and though his examples are military – 'bodyguards, Pretorians, "red" or "white" guards'[69] – the concept can apply equally to an administrative or bureaucratic elite. But a distinction can be made within a distinction, not only between the ruling group and the ruled, but within the ruling group between leader and immediate supporters and staff. In autocratic regimes where there are no settled mechanisms for changing rulers, and where such change will occur only through coup or rebellion, the boundaries between ruler and staff will blur. In representative electoral systems with distinctive bureaucracies the distinction within the governing elite will be clearer. Whilst the officials may, particularly at the most senior levels, be partisan appointments who change when governments change in response to electoral choices, there will frequently be a larger or smaller relative number of officials whose tenure is not dependent on the results of elections, who display a degree of non-partisan neutrality, and whose loyalty is to an identity – professional, constitutional, national, professional, state – distinct from that of party.

But the distinction between ruler and immediate staff is equally valid for regimes formally governed by a single ruler. No one can rule alone, and government is in all cases an activity carried out by at least one hierarchy and frequently several overlapping hierarchies of governors who, whatever their ostensible status as leaders, administrative staff, soldiers, or advisers, are all engaged in a common enterprise. Whether the regime is representative and democratic, monarchic, or a one-party autocracy, rulers need to legitimate themselves not only in their own eyes, but in the eyes of their immediate staff, whilst ruler and staff collectively need to legitimate themselves to themselves. However the differentiation is applied, four aspects of legitimation are observable. Rulers are legitimating themselves in their own eyes; at the same time they are legitimating themselves in the sight of their immediate supporters – administrators, advisers, military leaders; the governing community is legitimating itself collectively in its own eyes; and the governing community is legitimating itself in the eyes of ordinary subjects. 'When legitimation comes from the top', Guiseppi di Palma argues, 'the decisive operative relationship is not that between rulers and people, but

[69] Weber, *Economy and Society*, p. 214.

that between rulers and Weber's administrative staff – in communist parlance, the *cadres*.[70] The point is similar to one made by T. H. Rigby, also talking about communist European systems of government before 1989, when he writes that 'even in cases where the system of rule is so assured of dominance that its claim to legitimacy plays little or no part in the relationship between rulers and subjects, the mode of legitimation retains its significance as the basis for the relation of authority between rulers and administrative staff and for the structure of rule'.[71] The observation can be applied equally to the case of China under Mao Xedong, of which Frederick Teiwes comments that 'the acceptance of the leader's legitimacy by his high-ranking colleagues is *the* crucial factor for survival in Leninist systems'.[72] In regimes with 'princes' of one kind or another, the loyalty of courtiers is essential, and systematically cultivated, in a way that that of ordinary subjects may not be.[73] Nor are princes confined to monarchies. The method of addressing Mao Xedong bore strong similarities to the method of addressing emperors, as the prostrate prose of the defence minister addressing his leader in 1959 illustrates: 'I am a simple man . . . and indeed I am crude and have not tact at all. For this reason, whether this letter is of reference value or not is for you to decide. If what I say is wrong, please correct me.'[74]

But whilst relations within the sphere of government may be of primary importance, distinctions within the sphere of government are conversely of far less significance than distinctions between the community of governors and the rest of the population. If rulers and those immediate followers and administrators who participate in their rule employ human mirrors for their self-creation, they provide those mirrors for each other as much as they seek them amongst the mass of citizens, voters, or subjects. The

[70] Guiseppe Di Palma, 'Legitimation From the Top to Civil Society: Politico-Cultural Change in Eastern Europe', *World Politics* 44, 1 (October 1991), 49–80, p. 57.
[71] T. H. Rigby, 'Introduction: Political Legitimacy, Weber and Communist Mono-organisational Systems' in T. H. Rigby and Ferenc Féher (eds.), *Political Legitimation in Communist States* (New York, St. Martin's Press, 1982), p. 15.
[72] Frederick C. Teiwes, *Leadership, Legitimacy, and Conflict in China: From a Charismatic Mao to the Politics of Succession* (London, Macmillan, 1984), p. 45. Italics in the original.
[73] At the court of Louis XIV, 'for the courtiers, especially the higher nobility' attendance at court was 'virtually compulsory', Burke, *The Fabrication of Louis XIV*, p. 153.
[74] Teiwes, *Leadership, Legitimacy, and Conflict in China*, p. 66.

origins of the fusion of royal and saintly identities in a Westminster Abbey which celebrated both Edward the Confessor and the Plantagenets lay 'somewhere within the specific institutional circles which had nurtured the saint's reputation in the first place, namely the Benedictines of Westminster and, perhaps, the immediate circle of the king. There never was, and never would be, a popular cult.'[75]

But just as autocratic rulers can be at least as dependent in their legitimation on their administrative staff as representative ones, so representative rulers, who because of their election might seem to have less need to justify themselves, legitimate themselves within the secret garden of government as energetically as do princes and despots. There may be less difference than at first appears between monarchical and other absolute institutions of governments, and democratic, liberal, representative and constitutional ones. It might appear that the leadership of the latter is collective, that of the former single or individual. But the solitary ruler is Alexander Selkirk or King Lear, not a reigning monarch. There is a necessary extension of even absolute rule beyond the immediate person of the king, president, or general, just as, by contrast, there is a contraction of democracy into the inner circle of the representative ruler. But, in each case, legitimation is both collective and social, and individually experienced.

LEADERS AND LED IN NATIONALISM

One instance which might seem seriously to qualify the claim that rulers justify themselves to themselves as much if not more so than they do to or in the sight of those whom they rule, is provided by nationalist regimes. The leadership it might be argued justifies itself continuously to its following, and its principal claim is that it represents that following. Legitimation is almost entirely exogenous rather than endogenous, there is little if any self-referential justification, and there is an overwhelming emphasis on the link between the people and their leaders. It is a claim which has been subject to severely sceptical review by, in different ways, Russell

---

[75] Binski, *Westminster Abbey and the Plantagenets*, p. 3.

Hardin who speaks of parasitic leaders, and Aijiz Ahmad, who argues that national and ethnic identity is a myth exploited by a few politicians and opportunists.[76] There are good initial reasons to be sceptical of the national or ethnic claim of leaders to speak for a community of equals. As a form of legitimation, nationalism familiarly presents the leader, party, soldier, or revolutionary as the representative of the nation, the culture of the community or patria politically expressed. Nationalism seeks exceptional representatives of its mundane virtues, and has a long history of fondness for heroes. Eric Hobsbawm comments on Miroslav Hroch's three-stage model of nationalism, where it is only in the third stage that the nationalist elite turns to and enlists the masses, that the 'official ideologies of states and movements are not guides to what is in the minds of even the most loyal citizens or supporters'.[77] But one might reply that that indicates not so much the importance of the neglected people, as their relative unimportance.

There are two dimensions of elitism involved in nationalism. First, it is the elite which most fully represents the nation, which expresses its distinctive character more fully than do ordinary people. At a time of national danger or crisis, the nation's interests are frequently invested in one outstanding individual, to whose judgements ordinary people must defer. When W. J. M. Mackenzie commented of the subtitle of a book by Lucien Pye, *Burma's Search for Identity*, that '"Burma" is in no position to search for an identity unless it already has one',[78] the point was not, at least potentially, simply negative. 'Burma' may not have been searching for an identity, but somebody must have been. Princes and potentates, or publicists and politicians, stand in for fictional communities on such occasions.

Second, not only do an elite or a leader normally possess the magic symbols of nationalism, but the national message is directed with especial force and articulacy to a minority. The greater the numbers involved in its reception, the less frequently is the message

[76] Aijaz Ahmad, *In Theory: Classes, Nations, Literatures* (London, Verso, 1992), pp. 287–318; Russell Hardin, *One for All: The Logic of Group Conflict* (Princeton, NJ, Princeton University Press, 1995).
[77] Eric Hobsbawm, *Nations and Nationalism since 1780: Programme, Myth, Reality* (Cambridge, 1990), p. 11.
[78] W. J. M. Mackenzie, *Political Identity* (Harmondsworth: Penguin, 1978), p. 30.

transmitted and the less its articulacy and complexity. This means that many of the standard accounts miss the point: nationalism is not only expressive of the values of an elite, it expresses those values principally *to* an elite.

Is not this, however, simply an occasional feature of some nationalisms, rather than a regular characteristic of all? Do not twentieth-century totalitarian regimes represent a different use of nationalism, aimed principally at the masses? Is this not one of the ways in which they differ from simple despotisms? Totalitarian regimes have certainly directed a lot more propaganda at the masses than have other kinds of regime. But the employment of nationalist legitimation for and within the elite is also, correspondingly, increased. It is not, in other words, the relative distribution of nationalist messages of legitimacy which is changed in such regimes, but the overall volume or amount of those messages. The nationalist propaganda of Nazi Germany was considerable, and in some cases apparently specifically designed for mass consumption. Leni Reifenstahl's *Triumph of the Will* was not so much a film of a party rally, as a film for which the rally was specifically stage managed. The organisation of the rally was a part of the creation of the film, and the ritual for the party elite was subordinated to the creation of images for mass consumption. But the closer one went to the heart of the Nazi regime, the greater the amount of time and effort that was spent on legitimation. Members of the SS spent far more time on Nordic flummery than ever did the ordinary subject of Nazi Germany.[79] Totalitarian regimes were in this respect typical of a far wider spectrum of regimes. In even the most liberal and democratic regimes, presidents spend a greater proportion of their time at formal, and closed, occasions of one kind and another – banquets, receptions, ceremonies, ritual *tête-à-têtes* with visiting dignitaries – than ever they do on walkabouts in the street or the supermarket. Totalitarian or populist nationalism is in this respect not so different from democratic or constitutional versions. As the central symbol of English or British nationalism, the larger part of the rituals and ceremonials in which the queen participates are relatively or completely private. But since the queen is not a major political player,

[79] Kertzer, *Ritual, Politics, and Power*, pp. 163–7.

these activities are significant as legitimation, not for her, but for others on whom she confers, or mirrors, the dignity of office.

FORMS OF LEGITIMATION AND FORMS OF GOVERNMENT

One corrective to an impression of similarity in a ubiquitous self-legitimation by rulers is provided by Weber's suggestion about the relation between the manner in which rulers legitimate themselves and the manner of their rule. This frequently overlooked relationship is presented as organic rather than mechanical or evidently causal. It is of particular relevance at a time when worries are being expressed amongst political scientists about the legitimation of the European Union, and the governance of the European Union is considered by many to show serious flaws. Most such discussion has been of the ways in which those subject to the government of the European Union might be normatively persuaded to comply. The problem described has been how to legitimate subjecthood. What has not been considered is the importance of legitimation not for obedience or loyalty amongst citizens of the European Union, but in shaping, restraining, and sustaining the manner of governance. The question that is then raised is not, 'Is the European Union legitimate?' but 'What is associated with the particular ways in which it legitimates itself?' The European Union Commission in the period leading up to the mass resignation of commissioners in March 1999 was not endogenously *un*-legitimated. But it was legitimated in a way which sustained, and was sustained by, unaccountability, high self-regard which was not supported by any reference to polity, citizens, or representatives, secrecy and lack of publicity, and a largely inwardly referring referential framework. 'What is relevant is the image one has about oneself, and about the policy one is making ... That is what public interest is. Outside influences do not weigh (very much).'[80] In other words, in terms of Weber's observed occurrence and function of legitimation, legitimation was in the

---

[80] 'Official 058', quoted in Liesbet Hooghe, 'Images of Europe', p. 364; cf. Helen Wallace, 'Deepening and Widening: Problems of Legitimacy for the EC', in Soledad Garcia (ed.), *European Identity and the Search for Legitimacy* (London, Pinter, 1993), p. 97: 'Reforms were made periodically to the EC and its institutions. These did add to the trappings of democratic form, but marginally so, leaving the patrician and technocratic processes predominant.'

first place internal to government, not external. It was part of how government was conducted, not part of the relations it had with those whom it governed.[81] But the manner of legitimation and the character of government will be organically related.

THE FAILURE OF SELF-LEGITIMATION

Self-legitimation is necessary for rulers. The legitimation of the unique identity of governers, and the legitimation of governers by the enactment of their unique identity, is part of the continual rationalisation of rule. When this fails, government fails, it in fact ceases to be government. A range of instances of this can be found in studies of communist regimes in Eastern Europe both in and before 1989, which see the loss of confidence, the failure of self-justification of rulers, as the key element. Well before the collapse, in 1977, Joseph Rothschild argued that the importance of the self-legitimation of ruling elites had been ignored: 'Discussions of legitimacy and legitimation risk irrelevancy if they overlook this crucial dimension of a ruling elite's sense of its legitimacy and focus exclusively on the other dimension of the public's or the masses' perceptions of that elite's legitimacy.'[82] Five years before the events of 1989, Paul Lewis was suggesting that 'it is elite disintegration and the failure of its internal mechanisms of authority that have engendered the more general collapse of legitimacy and the onset of political crises in communist Eastern Europe'.[83] In a discussion of East Germany in 1984, Martin McCaulcy wrote of 'the self-defined or self-ascriptive legitimacy based on the writings of Marx and Engels. If the umbilical cord linking the SED to Marx were cut, the party would wither away.'[84] A similar view was expressed at the same time by Jan Pakulski who argued that 'Doctrinal consensus and the sense of legitimacy play a crucial

[81] I have left aside here the question of whether, or in what sense, institutions such as the European Union can be considered as governments.
[82] J. Rothschild, 'Observations on Political Legitimacy in Contemporary Europe', *Political Science Quarterly* 92, 3 (1977), 487–501, p. 491.
[83] Paul G. Lewis (ed.), 'Legitimation and Political Crises: East European Developments in the Post-Stalin Period' in Paul G. Lewis (ed.), *Eastern Europe: Political Crisis and Legitimation*, pp. 1–41 (London, Croom Helm, 1984), p. 35.
[84] Martin McCauley (ed.), 'Legitimation in the German Democratic Republic' in Lewis (ed.), *Eastern Europe*, p. 63.

role in unifying elites and cementing the links between the leaders and the political-administrative apparata.[85] With the collapse of communist regimes across Eastern Europe in 1989, Pakulski was able to apply the general point to the Polish example: 'Ideological disintegration of the elite-apparatus and the loss of Soviet support heralded the collapse of the regime and started a massive social transformation.'[86] Such accounts presented the events of 1989 as an internal failure, rather than principally the result of external, popular pressure. Leslie Holmes summed up the argument in retrospect. 'If the whole, or at least most of the key elements, of the elite loses faith in what it is doing and in the very system it is supposed to maintain – if there is near-universal collapse of self-legitimation – then the fourth form of legitimation crisis has occurred. In many ways, this concept provides one of the most important and persuasive explanations of the collapse of communism.'[87]

Such an account of the collapse of communist regimes in Eastern Europe in 1989 departs from the democratic assumptions of much political science. There are two counter-narratives. The first, the relatively weaker response, argues that the loss of self-confidence in the ruling elite was vital, but that the elite lost confidence only because of popular protest. An interesting application of this insight can be found in the discussion, though not in the arguments, of Jan Kubik, who suggests that the development of counter-legitimations by opposition groups in Poland before 1989 facilitated the change of policy by the communist ruling group.[88] The second and stronger response is that the elite's loss of self-confidence was no more than a registering of a notice of dismissal that had already effectively been delivered by the people, so was of no consequence. A third, and subtle, variant is the argument that the elite's loss of confidence can actually stimulate the development of counter-legitimations.

[85] Jan Pakulski, 'Ideology and Political Domination: A Critical Re-appraisal', *International Journal of Comparative Sociology* 28, 3–4 (1987), 129–57, p. 150.

[86] Jan Pakulski, 'Poland: Ideology, Legitimacy and Political Domination' in Nicholas Abercrombie, Stephen Hill, and Bryan S. Turner (eds.), *Dominant Ideologies* (London, Unwin Hyman, 1990), p. 58; cf. Jan Pakulski, 'East European Revolutions and "Legitimacy Crisis"' in Janina Frentzel-Zagórska (ed.), *From a One-Party State to Democracy*, 67–87 (Amsterdam, Rodopi, 1993).

[87] Leslie Holmes, *Post-Communism: An Introduction* (Cambridge, Polity, 1997), p. 53.

[88] Jan Kubik, *The Power of Symbols against the Symbols of Power: The Rise of Solidarity and the Fall of State Socialism in Poland* (Pennsylvania, Pennsylvania State University Press, 1994).

Mancur Olson argues somewhat along these lines, not with respect to the mass of the population, but with respect to the middle and lower-range officials of the regime. If these arms and legs of the regime lose confidence in it, then the way is open for control to evaporate. 'Accordingly, when there is a successful insurrection against an autocratic regime, I hypothesize that it is normally due to the problems, divisions, irresolutions, or other weaknesses of the regime, not because of an increase in the animosity of the population.'[89]

The implications of these arguments might seem to be discouraging for democrats, though advocates of a broadly democratic theory of legitimation such as David Beetham and Christopher Lord have given them guarded acknowledgement.[90] But the discouragement is more apparent than real. Democratic protests were clearly an element in the events of 1989, and Di Palma has offered consolation to democrats by arguing that regimes which are self-legitimating, and which lack popular normative support, which are not democratically legitimated, are uniquely vulnerable.[91] What Di Palma calls legitimation from the top is, he argues, a distinctive form of legitimation, found in regimes which cannot convincingly claim that they have emerged or been sustained as a result of democratic choice.[92] But a different observation is that legitimation from the top is a feature of all regimes, not just of despotisms. There is then a gradient of legitimation and identification, and the confidence, and the crises of confidence, are more important the closer the heart of the activity of government is approached. If legitimacy is more important for rulers than for subjects and citizens, so is the collapse of legitimacy. The failure or weakening of legitimation becomes

[89] Mancur Olson, 'The Logic of Collective Action in Soviet-type Societies', *Journal of Soviet Nationalities* 1 (Summer 1990), 8–27, pp. 15–16.
[90] Beetham and Lord, *Legitimacy and the European Union*, p. 10: 'Analysts of political legitimacy from Max Weber onwards have argued about whether the recognition or acknowledgement of a regime's legitimacy is only important to the behaviour of its elites or administrative staff, rather than of subjects more widely. Naturally, any regime is particularly dependent on the co-operation of its own officials, and their acknowledgment of its authority is therefore especially important. Yet it is rare in the contemporary world for subjects to be so powerless that a regime can dispense with any wider claims to legitimacy.' The use of the word 'rare' is a small qualification through which a major qualification of the argument could intrude.
[91] Di Palma, 'Legitimation from the Top to Civil Society', pp. 56–7.
[92] Ibid., pp. 56–7.

more important the further up the institutional tree one climbs. All regimes are characterised by legitimation from the top, and all rulers therefore suffer when top-down legitimation, endogenous self-legitimation, fails. Legitimation and the collapse of legitimation may affect the allegiance of subjects. It is crucial to the internal health and survival of ruling groups. The most serious legitimacy crisis for any group of rulers will be that which occurs, not amongst its subjects, but amongst its own ranks. Regimes can survive an absence, failure or collapse of legitimation amongst their subjects.[93] They cannot survive a collapse of legitimation within the personnel of government. When subjects lose faith in rulers, government becomes difficult. When rulers lose confidence in themselves, it becomes impossible.

IS LEGITIMATION A PRIVATE GAME?

If there is a form of legitimation carried on away from the public gaze, and for the satisfaction of rulers rather than of subjects, is this activity any more than a private game of government? Does it have any consequences for either the way in which government is conducted or its impact on those who are ruled by it? The question has been raised in a related context by David Cannadine, when he asks of his own jointly edited collection of studies of royal ritual, 'But to what end? To say of pomp and pageantry that there has always been a great deal of it about, and here are some more examples, albeit from unusually exotic locations, is not of itself particularly significant.'[94] There are two principal answers. The first is that any activity to which humans devote a regular and significant amount of attention is prima facie of importance for students of human society. Time, energy, and resources go on what, from a limited

[93] J. Pakulski, 'Legitimacy and Mass Compliance: Reflections on Max Weber and Soviet-Type Societies', *British Journal of Political Science*, 16, 1 (1986), 35–56; Pakulski, 'Poland'; J. Pakulski, 'Ideology and Political Domination: A Critical Re-appraisal', *International Journal of Comparative Sociology* 28, 3–4 (1987), 129–57; N. Abercrombie and B. S. Turner, 'The Dominant Ideology Thesis' in Anthony Giddens and David Held (eds.), *Classes, Power, and Conflict: Classical and Contemporary Debates* (London, 1982); Abercrombie, Hill, and Turner (eds.), *Dominant Ideologies*; J. Rothschild, 'Political Legitimacy in Contemporary Europe' in B. Denitch (ed.), *Legitimation of Regimes: International Frameworks for Analysis* (Beverley Hills, Sage, 1979).
[94] Cannadine, 'Introduction: Divine Rites of Kings', p. 12.

perspective, is a non-functional aspects of government. But the judgement of non-functionality is deductive not inductive. The raw material, in such an instance, sets the perimeters of the enquiry, and not vice versa. The second answer is that since government is a game with public consequences, it matters very much how it is carried on, with what justifications, self-descriptions, and hoped for or believed in identifications. Looking at government from the centre outwards by focusing on endogenous legitimation, the self-legitimation of rulers, will not give a 'correct' account, nor will it supersede 'incorrect' accounts, but it will add an extra dimension, and give a fuller, more rounded, description.

But however self-regarding the legitimation of rulers may be, they do not act alone. If they did so, they would not be rulers. The difference between a king in office and a king in exile is that the latter has no subjects. There are not only subjects, but mighty subjects who demand particular attention, and rebels who engage in a legitimation of their own, as well as ordinary subjects who are never entirely excluded. Their relation to the legitimation of rulers, and their own identifications and legitimations will be considered in the remaining chapters.

CHAPTER 4

Cousins at home and abroad

CIRCLES AND HIERARCHIES

At the beginning of the twentieth century the reigning and ruling families of Britain, Norway, Romania, Sweden, Germany, Greece, and Russia were all related by blood or marriage. A monarch in one country could look to the head of state in another and recognise at one remove or another, a cousin. A hundred years later things might seem to have been transformed. The disappearance of monarchy over much of the world has brought to an end the familial links between governments. But the informal fraternity of the powerful, and their mutual sustaining of each other's identities and status, has continued. And just as royal families had cousins both at home and abroad in the form of mighty subjects and rulers of states, so non-royal rulers engage in mutual legitimation with 'cousins' both amongst their own subjects, and amongst the rulers of other states. Courts are not a monopoly of royalty, nor is a private world of mutual identity confirmation the preserve of an aristocracy.

Legitimation by rulers for the confirmation of their own identity and authority is carried on in a series of concentric circles. It takes place first at the centre, and for the benefit of the immediate ruler or rulers. Then it takes place at one remove from the centre, both between ruler and staff, and amongst the staff themselves. Next it takes place in an exchange between the ruling group as a whole or some of its members, and the cousins, the members of the ruling groups in other states and the mighty subjects who stand nearer to the throne or the presidential palace than do ordinary subjects or citizens, and at some distance from the street, the factory, or the forum. Finally, legitimation takes place between rulers and their staff either collectively or individually, and more probably individually, and subjects and citizens as a whole. At each stage out from the centre it is likely to be carried out with less time, attention, energy and intensity, though at any stage the investment can be greater than a narrow utilitarian view would lead one to expect or could obviously explain. And, at each stage, the legitimation is reciprocal.

Because legitimation confirms and cultivates identity, when government legitimates itself in communication with cousins, the prestige of the cousins is enhanced at the same time.[1] Because rulers seek to confirm their particular form of identity and prestige, they legitimate themselves both downwards and sideways. This legitimation, which is both external, in communication with other states and other rulers, and internal, in communication with the rulers' own mighty subjects, works to cultivate and sustain the identities of all parties to it.[2]

INTERNAL COUSINS: ELITES

Rulers, in order to sustain and cultivate their own identity and authority, sustain and cultivate not only their own but that of those they recognise as marked off from the mass of their subjects by identities which attach them to both other individuals and groups, and raise them above them as leaders, representatives, and spokespersons. This has been frequently depicted by those discussing the powers and strategies of rulers as a means for them to legitimate themselves in the eyes of the whole body of those whom they govern. Heisler and Kvavik comment that the 'legitimation of outputs emanating from the decision-making sub-system is greatly facilitated by the cooptation of important groups or sectoral actors (while the particular identities of such actors are sustained or

---

[1] The support of significant others as described by Arthur Stinchcombe is thus a two-way process. The significant others can benefit just as can rulers. Arthur L. Stinchcombe, *Constructing Social Theories* (New York, Harcourt Brace, 1968), pp. 150–1, 158–63.

[2] The 'leadership maintains its sense of self-confidence and legitimacy by engaging in continuous efforts to gain the support of other individuals and groups wherever they may be found inside or outside the territorial limits of a claimed territorial and supposedly national or at least consensus-oriented jurisdiction', Arthur J. Vidich, 'Legitimation of Regimes in World Perspective' in Arthur J. Vidich and Ronald M. Glassman (eds.), *Conflict and Control: Challenges to Legitimacy of Modern Governments*, 271–302 (London, Sage, 1979), p. 295.

even reinforced, rather than challenged)'.[3] This can involve either
incorporation or delegation, whereby, 'Authority to formulate and
implement public policy has been delegated in substantial degree to
the administrative subsystem which, in turn, has passed some of its
responsibilities to the "private sector".'[4] But a problem for such an
account lies in the co-option of discrete groups. How can this assist
legitimation as an exchange between rulers and subjects? Why does
not the seemingly privileged association of some persons with government alienate everyone else? Particularly in democracies, why
does not a special relationship with government for some, offend
the egalitarian expectations of the majority, especially if that relationship not only rewards the distinctive identities of a minority, but
leads to those identities being 'sustained or even reinforced'? Philip
Selznick responds to this difficulty by arguing that such cooption
must be concealed or at least veiled. 'If adjustment to specific nu-
cleuses of power becomes public, then the legitimacy of the formal
authority, as representative of a theoretically undifferentiated community (the "people as a whole"), may be undermined. It therefore
becomes useful and often essential for such coöptation to remain
in the shadowland of informal interaction.'[5] But the problem may
be one that is suggested by democratic expectations as much as
by historical evidence. A contractual or representative democratic
theory could lead to the expectation that government is at all times,
or predominantly, representative of the whole people. Discrete
legitimating or representative relations with particular groups
would infringe the principles incorporated in such a theory. But
it is less clear that in observable historical instances popular or
widespread disaffection or dissatisfaction arises from such varied,
particular, and partial relationships. Further, the phrasing of the difficulty assumes that the function of legitimation for governments is
the maintenance of support amongst ordinary subjects. But if that
is not the case, and if a significant feature of legitimation is the confirmation and cultivation of the identity of rulers themselves, then

[3] M. O. Heisler and Robert B. Kvavik, 'Patterns of European Politics: The "European
Polity" Model' in M. O. Heisler (ed.), *Politics in Europe: Structures and Processes in Some
Postindustrial Democracies*, 27–89 (New York, David McKay, 1974), p. 23.

[4] Ibid., pp. 22–3.

[5] Philip Selznick, 'Coöptation: A Mechanism for Organizational Stability' in R. K. Merton
(ed.), *Reader in Bureaucracy*, 135–9 (Glencoe, IL, Free Press of Glencoe, 1964), pp. 136–7.

the partial or select character of its legitimation dialogues has a different importance.

The reciprocal nature of the exchange is an aspect not just of relations between states and elites whose character and identity are given at the start of the relationship and unchanged by it, but of the development and formation of the identities of each side. Just as monarchs can create aristocrats, so can governments call 'cousins' into existence. Michael Saward comments that 'co-optees are not always drawn from "constituted" groups, and indeed . . . can be created, incorporated and their leaders co-opted as barely separable parts of the same state action'.[6] Cooption and endorsement by government are aspects of a single process giving reciprocal advantages and influencing reciprocal identities. Marc Raeff comments that

classes (in the Marxist sense of groups defined by their members' role and interests in the prevailing modes of production rather than by their social status and function) were the result of the encouragement and stimulation provided by the initiatives of the well-ordered *Polizeistaat*. By intervening in the daily activities of its subjects and by fostering the maximum utilization of all resources and creative energies, the absolutist state undermined the estate structure, on which it often relied in practice and promoted the dynamics of modernization and the formation of classes.[7]

A similar function, though a deliberate rather than an almost accidental one, has been attributed to the state in its creation of property rights. Margaret Levi follows Douglass C. North in this, and quotes him on the way in which rulers are to be observed 'separating each group of constituents and devising property rights for each so as to maximize state revenue'.[8]

---

[6] Michael Saward, *Co-optive Politics and State Legitimacy* (Aldershot, Dartmouth, 1992), p. 23.

[7] Marc Raeff, 'The Well-Ordered Police State and the Development of Modernity in Seventeenth- and Eighteenth-Century Europe: An Attempt at a Comparative Approach', *American Historical Review* (1975), 1128.

[8] Douglass C. North, *Structure and Change in Economic History* (New York, W. W. Norton, 1981), p. 23, quoted in Margaret Levi, *Of Rule and Revenue* (London, 1988), p. 10. The work of Levi and of North is part of a wider insistence within political science that government should be seen not only as active and initiating, but as influencing, shaping, and creating the society upon which it works. Patrick Dunleavy's criticisms of Anthony Downs are thus part of this wider tradition, Patrick Dunleavy, *Democracy, Bureaucracy and Public Choice: Economic Explanations in Political Science* (Hemel Hempstead, Harvester Wheatsheaf, 1991), pp. 102–5. The selling of shares in publicly owned enterprises by the Conservative governments in Britain between 1979 and 1997 can be seen as an attempt, amongst other things,

The cultivation by government of identities amongst its more powerful subjects can be informal or formal. Informal instances can frequently fit Selznick's model of tactical secrecy. Patrick Dunleavy comments on the secrecy which characterises dealings between government and selected businesses and organisations in relationships whereby government 'can offer favourable treatment to the leading representative organisation and help to promote it as the sole legitimate spokesman of the industry. In return, the Department gains a simplified external environment and demands "responsible conduct" from the interest group.'[9] A formal instance, involving incorporation and legal regulation is provided by the cultivation of professional identities. The development of professions, which has sometimes been presented as a competition for power between private associations and the state, can be seen more convincingly as a collaborative, though negotiated and contested, relationship from which each party can benefit, and by which each is shaped. One of the functions of professional organisations is to regulate entry into the occupation, and if they are to do that, they require 'institutions endowed with authority' and the 'most important source of that authority is the state'.[10] But each side can gain from such development, and the history of both medicine and law in the United Kingdom, and elsewhere, is one of the creation and cultivation and modification of professions in association with the reciprocally changing financial, administrative, and legislative powers of government.[11] In that association each side has its identity

---

to create or cultivate a group who saw themselves as investors with a stake in a market economy, and for whom a Conservative government was thus compatible. The creation of a sense of identity as shareholders was to this extent of greater importance than the actual distribution of shares, and was not vitiated by the fact that a decreasing proportion of shares were in fact in private hands.

[9] Patrick Dunleavy, 'Quasi-governmental Professionalism: Some Implications for Public Policy-making in Britain' in Anthony Barker (ed.), *Quangos in Britain: Government and the Networks of Public Policy Making* (London, Macmillan, 1982), p. 189.

[10] Margaret Brazier, Jill Lovecy, Michael Moran, and Margaret Potton, 'Falling from a Tightrope: Doctors and Lawyers Between the Market and the State', *Political Studies* 41, 2 (June 1993), 197.

[11] 'the professions are emergent as a condition of state formation and state formation is a major condition of professional autonomy', T. Johnson, 'The State and the Professions: Peculiarities of the British' in Anthony Giddens and G. Mackenzie (eds.), *Social Class and the Division of Labour: Essays in Honour of Ilya Neustadt*, 186–208 (Cambridge, Cambridge University Press, 1982), p. 189.

legitimated, not as a static and merely acknowledged status, but as an actively developed consciousness whose importance is not principally dependent on the publicity or otherwise of the legitimation, but on its simple enactment.

MUTUAL SUPPORT

The pattern of legitimation in which cousins and rulers sustain and cultivate their legitimating identities is similar in this respect to the wider patterning of social order and command. Feudalism provides an intense example of a hierarchy where authority passed down from one rank to the next, and where the rituals of allegiance and alliance confirmed the identity and status of each party. The patterns of legitimation exchange in a wide range of societies both told people who they were, and in so doing, told them how they were distinguished from others. Norbert Elias comments on the members of the 'court society' of the *ancien régime* that: 'In their etiquette, too, they did not come together for etiquette's sake. To enact their existence, to demonstrate their prestige, to distance themselves from lower-ranking people and have this distance recognized by the higher-ranking – all this was purpose enough in itself. But in etiquette this *distancing of oneself from others as an end in itself* finds its consummate expression.'[12] The progression of visitors to the royal presence at Versailles was through a series of courts, vestibules, and courtyards of increasing grandeur and remoteness.[13] Each stage announced and dramatised the identity of both parties. The grandeur of monarchic, as of totalitarian, courts, might seem to make them a case apart from other types of rule and rulers. But within the distinguishing extravagance of the manner of expression is a far from unique mode of identification and authorisation. The courts of the *ancien régime* and the utopian settlements of nineteenth-century industrial philanthropy, for instance, shared functional parallels. Social order in the nineteenth-century model industrial township of Saltaire was reproduced, symbolised, and sustained by a pattern of streets and houses with the manager at the centre, and each

[12] Norbert Elias, *The Court Society*, trans. Edmund Jephcott (1st edn 1969; Oxford, Blackwell, 1983), pp. 100–1.
[13] Ibid.

street ordered by the corner-capping houses of the foremen. The distance of mighty subjects from ordinary citizens and subjects is as important for their cultivation and confirmation of their own identity as is their closeness to rulers and governors. Rituals of inclusion and exclusion are a part of the conversation between rulers and cousins, by which the special identity of each is confirmed.[14] The rituals of death can be as effective as those of life in this respect, confirming the status of participants in a funeral procession, and marking them off from the bulk of ordinary subjects.[15] And, in each case, since it is the difference from ordinary people that is being celebrated, cultivated, and confirmed, the participation, presence, or even awareness of ordinary people is not a central or even necessary part of the process.

THE PEOPLE ARE NOT THE PEOPLE

There is more interplay between governors and cousins than between government and subjects, and even when rulers or heads of state appear to be engaging in a public cultivation of their identity, the audience, even if numerous, can be anything but popular. Two celebratory nineteenth-century British paintings illustrate the point. Each shows a monarch visiting a part of the kingdom away from London, and, apparently, meeting the people. Each shows the monarch in the company of large numbers of non-royal persons. William IV is in a thronged square, Victoria on a dais facing a crowded assembly room. But closer attention shows that this is far from the case. Paintings of William IV in Lewes, and Victoria at the Imperial Exhibition in Glasgow, are each accompanied by charts identifying those assembled around the monarch.[16] In each

---

[14] Pierre Bourdieu comments of the investiture 'of a knight, Deputy, President of the Republic, etc.' that the 'act of institution is thus an act of communication, but of a particular kind: it *signifies* to someone what his identity is, but in a way that both expresses it to him and imposes it on him by expressing it in front of everyone . . . and thus informing him in an authoritative manner of what he is and what he must be': Pierre Bourdieu, ed. John B. Thompson, trans. Gino Raymond and A. Matthew, *Language and Symbolic Power* (Oxford, Polity, 1991), pp. 119, 121.

[15] Jennifer Woodward, *The Theatre of Death: The Ritual Management of Royal Funerals in Renaissance England, 1570–1625* (Woodbridge, Boydell Press, 1997), p. 24.

[16] A. Archer, *The Visit of King William IV and Queen Adelaide to Lewes, October 22nd 1830* (Lewes, Lewes Town Hall); Sir John Lavery, *The State Visit of Her Majesty Queen Victoria to the Glasgow Imperial Exhibition in 1888* (Glasgow, Scottish Royal National Concert Hall).

case, the crowd, or rather the company, consists of the local great and good: members of the aristocracy, clergy, officials, notables of one kind and another. And access to any wider public is difficult or barred by either the interior venue or the exterior barriers. Far from meeting the people, William and Victoria are meeting the very top layer, the governing layer, of local society. It is a meeting of symbolic head of state, and cousins, not of rulers and subjects. Because what was happening on such an occasion was the cultivation and affirmation of particular identities within a hierarchy of prestige, just as those who were present could feel assured in their sense of their rightful place amongst the elite, so those who were not present could feel excluded and affronted. A working-class member of one of Cambridge's friendly societies was offended that representatives of associations such as his were thought 'not good enough' to take part in a church procession in celebration of Queen Victoria's Diamond Jubilee in 1897.[17]

David Cannadine comments on this aspect of nineteenth-century British royal relations as a peculiar feature of the period when the monarchy was not held in particular esteem, and the means of public display were decayed or disappeared. Royal ritual, he nicely puts it, 'was not so much a jamboree to delight the masses, but a group right in which the aristocracy, the church and the royal family corporately re-affirmed their solidarity (or animosity) behind closed doors'.[18] But such restricted involvement in the legitimation of rulers was not a feature only of monarchies in low times. Ordinary subjects of Louis XIV might catch glimpses of him in public, but they did so only if they took the trouble to do so. The efforts of royal propagandists were not directed at them, but at a small minority of the population.[19] But when the formal or informal rulers or exercisers of sovereignty come out onto the public stage in more flamboyant monarchic times, or in more democratic ones, this does not of itself decrease the importance of the private one.

[17] Elizabeth Hammerton and David Cannadine, 'Conflict and Consensus on a Ceremonial Occasion: The Diamond Jubilee in Cambridge in 1897', *Historical Journal* 24, 1 (1981), 111–46, p. 143.
[18] David Cannadine, 'The Context, Performance and Meaning of Ritual: The British Monarchy and the "Invention of Tradition", c. 1820–1977' in Eric Hobsbawm and Terence Ranger (eds.), *The Invention of Tradition*, 101–64 (Cambridge, Cambridge University Press, 1983), p. 116.
[19] Peter Burke, *The Fabrication of Louis XIV* (New Haven, Yale University Press, 1992), pp. 156–7.

An increase in public display does not by any means necessarily complement a decrease in private display. Nor is the public the principal beneficiary or audience of either.

NATIONAL GROUPS, ETHNIC GROUPS, AND ELITES

The role of elites, of cousins, in maintaining regimes in power by either positive support or negative lack of opposition has been frequently documented. Mary Fulbrook, in discussing the history of Weimar Germany, observes that when 'elites fail to sustain that system – as in the Weimar Republic – it has little chance of success. When elites condone it, or acquiesce in it – however apparently unjust the system may be – then it has less chance of being brought down by internal unrest.'[20] The type of 'cousins' whom rulers legitimate and in interaction with whom they are legitimated will differ according to the kind of society being governed. Where civil society is repressed, or the kinds of associations that would constitute it are incorporated or formalised by law or bureaucracy or dominant party organisation, the 'cousins' will be correspondingly formalised. But they will still be ancillary to the actual governing groups, and distinguishable from them. In Eastern Germany before reunification, the Communist Party provided just such a formalisation of civil society, and its Central Committee performed functions analogous to those performed by presence at court in a monarchy. Membership was 'an emblem of having arrived'.[21] There was a mutual exchange of acknowledgement, or mirroring, of self-estimations, and membership 'reflects the top leadership's view of its own future composition but also concessions to the importance of different intraparty groups. In providing such group representation, it is a critical instrument of inner-party legitimacy.'[22] Societies with a less formally regulated structure, and characterised by ethnic, cultural, or religious pluralism will have their own distinctive cousins. But all such groups,

---

[20] Mary Fulbrook, *The Divided Nation: A History of Germany, 1918–1990* (Oxford, Oxford University Press, 1992), p. 9.

[21] Thomas S. Baylis, *The Technical Intelligentsia and the East German Elite: Legitimacy and Social Change under Mature Communism* (Berkeley, University of California Press, 1974), p. 188.

[22] Ibid., p. 189.

like rulers themselves, are likely to aspire to govern, whilst claiming to represent, those whom they define as their community or constituency. And all such groups, in making these claims, are open to the criticism that simultaneously to claim to represent a group or community, and to be distinguished from it by skill, advocacy, piety, or whatever quality, is to create a contradiction, of the kind that Gramsci attempted to resolve with the notion of the 'organic intellectual'.[23] As Jon Lawrence has argued in an examination of radical, socialist and labour politics in late nineteenth and early twentieth-century Britain, the organic activist, 'indistinguishable in every respect from his or her fellow workers', was 'no more than a romantic illusion; "representation" necessarily involves exclusion'.[24]

Thus the claims to identity and authority made on behalf of ethnic or cultural groups will seek to increase the influence which the leaders of those groups have over the community's members or claimed members. Karl Renner, speaking of nationalism as a self-ascribed status, could equally well have been talking of ethnic cultural, or other forms of group identity. It was, he wrote, 'freely chosen, *de jure*, by the individual who has reached the age of majority, and on behalf of minors, by their legal representatives'.[25] It is not only with regard to minors that such patriarchal assumptions are made.[26] It is for that reason that the state is so valuable to all manner of leaderships and aspirant leaderships. For whilst it may be true, as Hobsbawm puts it when speaking of nationalism, that 'nationalism comes before nations', he goes on to insist that

[23] Antonio Gramsci, *Selections from the Prison Notebooks of Antonio Gramsci*, ed. and trans. Quintin Hoare and Geoffrey Nowell Smith (London, Lawrence and Wishart, 1971); James Joll, *Gramsci* (London, Fontana/Collins, 1977).

[24] Jon Lawrence, *Speaking for the People: Party, Language and Popular Politics in England 1867–1914* (Cambridge, Cambridge University Press, 1998), p. 61.

[25] Karl Renner, Synopticus, *Staat und Nation* (Vienna 1899), pp. 7ff. quoted in Eric Hobsbawm, *Nations and Nationalism since 1780: Programme, Myth, Reality* (Cambridge, Cambridge University Press, 1990), p. 7.

[26] There is a conflict in contemporary discussion of cultural diversity between a tolerant pluralism which acknowledges the specificity of individual identity, and one which sees individuals as the bearers of group identity. Some of the problems of this are interestingly discussed by K. Anthony Appiah, 'Identity, Authenticity, Survival: Multicultural Societies and Social Reproduction' in Charles Taylor, *Multiculturalism: Examining The Politics of Recognition*, ed. and introduced by Amy Gutman, 2nd edn (Princeton, Princeton University Press 1994), p. 7.

'states and nationalisms' make nations.[27] The state, in other words, as an active and coercive institution, is essential to the creation of a nation, because of the exercise of cultural power or power over culture to which nationalism aspires and for which the state is its instrument.[28]

But this special place of elites in the various forms of legitimation is found in both nationalist and ethnic or cultural politics. The state is necessary to nationalism, but has too a vital role to play in the political identity of ethnic groups. The sustenance in their legitimation which rulers may gain by being seen as expressing the values of those whom they govern is not a one-way process. And whatever the differences between ethnic and national minorities, their relationship with the rulers is in this respect the same. In responding to national or ethnic minorities, rulers must find, or create, representatives who can speak for and thus also to an extent control 'their' communities. By seeking to sustain their own legitimation by alliances with national and ethnic minorities, rulers unavoidably confer status on and even create leaders and representatives, and at the same time contribute to the defining, sustaining, and creation of national and ethnic minorities. In sustaining or increasing their legitimation by their association with the representatives of groups of whatever kind within their territories, rulers at the same time increase or even confer the authority of those representatives both in their relations with other representatives of other groups, and in their dealings with those whom they claim to represent. Governors have an essential role in creating ethnic identities by recognising and sanctioning representatives and leaders – the national/ethnic aspect of corporatism. The place of central control within corporatism is not therefore a unique feature of its fascist form. Any dealings by rulers with the representatives of groups or communities assists those representatives not just in speaking for others, but

---

[27] Hobsbawm, *Nations and Nationalism since 1780*, p. 10.

[28] I am aware that a distinction is made between cultural nationalism and civic nationalism, and that what I am describing here is the former. In everyday language, however, the term nationalism usually refers to this first form. I do not intend to dismiss civic nationalism by omission, but rather to leave it on one side as a rather special, if valuable, form of nationalism which does not bear directly on the subject of this discussion.

in speaking to them and controlling and defining them.[29] When the east London socialist, trade unionist, and MP, Will Thorne, spoke of 'my people', the phrase conveyed 'the sense both of "my folk" and of "my subjects"'.[30]

Even when they recognise other communities than those from which they themselves traditionally spring, rulers recognise them in the persons of those who come closest to their own conception of order. In most countries this means they choose the patriarchs. So rulers, in dealing with groups within their territories, create and assist the power of elites. Nationalism and cultural pluralism has as one of its important aspects the claim to power over its alleged 'constituents' by an elite.[31] Both nationalists and ethnic minorities seek political power, and though this will be presented as power against an unrepresentative state, it will also be a claim to power over those who are seen by the national or cultural elite as part of 'their' community. This claim can be surprisingly intrusive. This is most obviously so within the private sphere of sexuality and gender relations, where it most frequently involves the claim of males to lay down the rules which should govern the conduct and aspirations of women and children, the distribution of power and status within the family and the church, and the forms of education and aspiration appropriate for males and females. This seems to be the direction in which Islamist Muslims in the United Kingdom are moving,[32] and in which churches of all faiths have frequently

[29] There is a substantial discussion within political theory over this aspect of pluralism, and about power *within* groups and associations. See, for instance, Will Kymlicka, *Multicultural Citizenship: A Liberal Theory of Minority Rights* (Oxford, Oxford University Press, 1995); Will Kymlicka (ed.), *The Rights of Minority Cultures* (Oxford, Oxford University Press, 1995); David Nicholls, *The Pluralist State: the Political Ideas of J. N. Figgis and His Contemporaries*, 2nd edn (London, Macmillan, 1994); Rodney Barker, 'Pluralism, revenant or recessive?' in J. Hayward, Brian Barry and Archie Brown (eds.), *The British Study of Politics in the Twentieth Century* (Oxford, Oxford University Press, 1999).

[30] Lawrence, *Speaking for the People*, p. 237.

[31] It is exactly this problem which has been the basis for criticisms of pluralism as a basis for constitutional representation. Who is to determine what is a group?

[32] I have used the term 'Islamist' rather than 'fundamentalist', the deficiencies of which have been widely pointed out. 'Islamist' indicates a desire to extend the prescriptions of faith into law and the coercive regulation of social and individual life. It is used in this sense by Fred Halliday, 'The Politics of Islam: A Second Look', *British Journal of Political Science* 25, 3 (July 1995).

moved. Thus, despite talk of a 'Muslim Parliament', the enterprise envisaged appears to have as much aspiration to control citizens, as to influence the state.[33] So Gilles Kepel argues that the protests in Yorkshire over the publication of Salman Rushdie's novel *The Satanic Verses* was a deliberate attempt by the local Muslim imams both to increase their influence with government and, by so doing, to increase their power within their own communities. In addition, their concern over *The Satanic Verses* was that in so far as Rushdie could be seen as having Muslim origins, the book, and the author, represented a dangerous example of an escape from community control: 'They had set themselves a precise aim: to establish themselves more firmly as intermediaries who could demand, as the price of social peace, concessions that would strengthen their communal position.'[34]

EXTERNAL COUSINS: STATES
AND INTERNATIONAL ORGANISATIONS

The German Reich Chancellery built in 1939 for Adolf Hitler created great distances and transitions from space to space which had to be traversed in order to reach the Führer's office. Charles Goodsell has pointed to the role of the Chancellery as a use of grand spaces to impress visitors.[35] But those visitors were not the public, the people, the subjects, but cousins of one kind and another, particularly foreign cousins, ambassadors, ministers, and politicians.

---

[33] The proposal in the late summer of 1990 was for a bi-cameral assembly, with a representative lower house of around 200 and an upper house composed of wealthy businessmen and professionals. One of the stated aims of such a body would be to give Muslims the kind of power or influence, the lack of which had prevented them securing the banning of *The Satanic Verses*, *The Glasgow Herald* (4 September 1990, p. 4). Subsequently, in the autumn of 1994, representatives of the Muslim Parliament commented publicly on the dispute arising from the proposed vaccination of children against measles, following the recommendation of the headmaster of Ampleforth, a private Roman Catholic boarding school, that because products from aborted foetuses had been used at stages of the production of the vaccination, Roman Catholic boys, but not Roman Catholic girls, should refuse vaccination.

[34] Gilles Kepel, *The Revenge of God: The Resurgence of Islam, Christianity and Judaism in the Modern World* (Cambridge, Polity, 1994), p. 39.

[35] Charles Goodsell, *The Social Meaning of Civic Space: Studying Political Authority through Architecture* (Lawrence, University Press of Kansas, 1988), p. 4.

Whilst rulers affirm their own identity and authority in their exchanges with internal, domestic cousins, they do so to an equal or greater extent with their governing peers, the rulers of other states. The meetings between Hitler and representatives of other governments, whether they were potential allies whom he wished to encourage, or possible enemies whom he wished to intimidate, were carefully and massively stage managed. Foreign relations are peer relations and have as one of their essential components the exchange of esteem, and the confirmation and cultivation of identity. But when Goodsell comments on the rituals conducted in civic space that their 'formalistic, solemn format reminds those who are present of the grand and even mysterious compulsion of state authority',[36] it is well to remember that even though the audience is likely to be small and select, the principal performer is more involved in the ceremony than any of them. Peter Burke has suggested that the presentation of Louis XIV, similarly, had three audiences: posterity, the upper classes of France, and foreigners.[37] But the ritual progressions which had filled the huge stage which was the Palace of Versailles did not depart with the *ancien régime* as the theatricals of the Berlin Chancellery show. In the Soviet Union, the reception of an ambassador was as choreographed as anything 300 years earlier, but was typical of rituals across a broad swathe of regimes where the elite of one regime had their importance confirmed by the elite of another. From the arrival of the ambassador, the officials who will speak, what they will say, on which side, left or right, they will stand, at what point they will appear, or disappear, were minutely set down. An order was prescribed for the presentation of credentials, the making of formal speeches, the welcomes, the handshakes, the moment of bowing, and the degree to which the head, in such a gesture, would be lowered.[38] Rulers habitually seek to impress those whom they regard as their peers with their own authority, and in so doing, confirm their own beliefs in their unique identity. It is not a form of legitimation which is restricted

---

[36] Ibid., p. 12.
[37] Burke, *Fabrication of Louis XIV*, p. 153.
[38] Thomas M. Franck, *The Power of Legitimacy Among Nations* (New York, Oxford University Press, 1990), pp. 107–8.

to monarchies or despotism. It may be expressed with jesters and jousting as when Henry VIII of England met Francis I of France at the Field of the Cloth of Gold in 1520,[39] or with the presentation of turkeys by President Eisenhower to a visiting Premier Khrushchev to illustrate the fecundity of American agriculture. The function is much the same.

Thomas Franck has argued that legitimating exchanges in international relations are the pure form of legitimacy, since there is no coercive context or sanction for laws or commands.[40] He describes a mutually legitimating relationship between the United Nations and individual states analogous to that which exists between national rulers and powerful groups or individuals within their own communities: 'The U.N., in voting to admit a new member, symbolically validates the status of a new state. At the same time, however, the U.N. manifests, and so reinforces, its own authority to bestow status by institutional acts of authentication.'[41] For the Eastern European communist leaderships in the years leading up to 1989, the approval of rulers of the Soviet Union provided a powerful confirmation of their governing roles, so that 'the leaders might still believe in their own right to rule because of direct or indirect external support, even though they are aware of their unpopularity and lack of authority among their own population'.[42] In Poland, the role of Marxism-Leninism as justificatory ideology for the leadership was thus crucial, not only in giving them an account of themselves, but in sustaining and mirroring that account in the eyes of the Soviet backers, 'in legitimizing the rulers in the eyes of their crucial external constituency – the Soviet leaders'.[43]

---

[39] Sydney Anglo, *Images of Tudor Kingship* (London, B. A. Seaby, 1992), pp. 30–4; Sydney Anglo, 'The Hampton Court Painting of the Field of the Cloth of Gold', *The Antiquaries Journal* 46 (1966), 287–307.

[40] Franck, *The Power of Legitimacy Among Nations*.

[41] Ibid., p. 96; cf. Michael N. Barnett, 'Bringing in the New World Order: Liberalism, Legitimacy, and the United Nations', *World Politics* 49, 4 (July 1997), 526–51; Inis Claude, Jr, 'Collective Legitimization as a Political Function of the United Nations', *International Organization* 20 (1966), 367–79.

[42] Leslie Holmes, *Post-Communism: An Introduction* (Cambridge, Polity, 1997), p. 45.

[43] Jan Pakulski, 'Poland: Ideology, Legitimacy and Political Domination' in Nicholas Abercrombie, Stephen Hill, and Bryan S. Turner (eds.), *Dominant Ideologies* (London, Unwin Hyman, 1990), p. 58; cf. Jan Pakulski, 'East European Revolutions and "Legitimacy Crisis"' in Janina Frentzel-Zagórska (ed.), *From a One-Party State to Democracy*, 67–87 (Amsterdam, Rodopi, 1993).

But legitimation is not to be understood only as a servant of power, or if it is the servant, it is the domestic chaplain not the secretary or the estate manager. The denial of appropriate recognition by other rulers can be the cause of intense unease or resentment, and whether from addiction to the pleasures of the knowledge of power, or from a need for the confirmation through legitimation of one's own governing identity, any apparent failure to accord proper recognition to what is perceived by one set of rulers as their status can lead to resentment, grievance, and complaint.[44] So the rulers of the Ottoman Empire 'found themselves increasingly obliged to assert their legitimate right to existence as a recognised member of the concert of Europe', and protested when it was felt that the Egyptian delegation was being given precedence at Queen Victoria's jubilee celebrations.[45] Their competitive desire for equal status would have been familiar in seventeenth-century Sweden engaging in self-assertive war,[46] or in ancient Rome, where ambassadors from German tribes, feeling themselves similarly overlooked, were reported to have taken unilateral action to sit in the seats assigned to those whose equals they wished to be considered.[47]

Like the rulers of nation-states, the principal actors in international or transnational institutions which exercise functions of government, legitimate themselves both within the community of their immediate colleagues, or in communication with their cousins. In the legal relations between states, 'law provides us not only with a means of adjudicating between right and wrong, but also with a way through which identities can be established, recognized, and developed'.[48] Similarly, in the institutional relations within

---

[44] Power can be its own reward, and the satisfaction of knowing one exercises it an autonomous source of pleasure or well-being. Robert E. Lane, 'Experiencing Money and Experiencing Power' in Ian Shapiro and Grant Reeher (eds.), *Power, Inequality, and Democratic Politics: Essays in Honour of Robert A. Dahl* (Boulder and London, Westview Press, 1988).

[45] Selim Deringil, *The Well-Protected Domains: Ideology and the Legitimation of Power in the Ottoman Empire, 1876–1909* (London, I. B. Tauris, 1998), pp. 3, 9–10.

[46] Erik Ringmar, *Identity, Interest and Action: A Cultural Explanation of Sweden's Intervention in the Thirty Years War* (Cambridge, Cambridge University Press, 1996).

[47] The incident is quoted by Thomas Franck from the account of Alberico Gentili, Franck, *Power of Legitimacy Among Nations*, p. 104.

[48] Erik Ringmar, 'The Relevance of International Law: A Hegelian Interpretation of a Peculiar Seventeenth Century Preoccupation', *Review of International Studies* 21 (1995), 87–103, p. 102.

organisations such as the European Union, there is a process that Helen Wallace describes as 'indirect legitimation via the political systems of the member states'. David Beetham and Christopher Lord similarly discuss the way in which the EU may be legitimated 'only indirectly via the political and administrative officials of its member states'.[49]

Like any other political body exercising jurisdiction, international institutions require justification in terms of the purposes or ends they serve, which cannot be met by other means, in this case by nation states themselves, or at the individual state level . . . Yet such justifications rarely percolate out beyond a narrow elite group; nor do they need to, it could be argued, since these institutions are not dependent on the cooperation of a wider public to effect their purposes. It is not the direct cooperation of ordinary citizens that is required to maintain the authority of the UN, of GATT, of NATO, etc., but that of the member states and their officials; and it is for the behaviour of these alone, therefore, that considerations of legitimacy are important.[50]

The qualification added by the use of the word 'rarely' opens the way to a much larger revision of both the general account, and the assessment of the relative roles of the political actors. Arthur Vidich had much earlier argued that in such circumstances 'the connection between legitimacy and consent or democracy breaks down completely'.[51] But it is clear from such accounts of the European Union that, whatever conclusions may be drawn in normative theory from such activities, there is a legitimation taking place which is endogenous and self-legitimating, rather than democratic or contractual.

Observing the high importance which is attached to the rituals and procedures of legitimation within the closed world of international cousins, students of politics and international relations have suggested various explanations for this investment of time and effort. The rites of legitimation, it has been suggested, are symbols, representing the reality of a state's existence. Clearly, rites which are

---

[49] Helen Wallace, 'Deepening and Widening: Problems of Legitimacy for the EC' in Soledad Garcia (ed.), *European Identity and the Search for Legitimacy* (London, Pinter, 1993), p. 97; Beetham and Lord, *Legitimacy and the European Union* (London, Longman, 1998), p. 10.

[50] Beetham and Lord, *Legitimacy and the European Union*, p. 12.

[51] Vidich, 'Legitimation of Regimes in World Perspective' in Vidich and Glassman (eds.), *Conflict and Control*, p. 301.

wholly out of accord with other realities will not function. Thomas Franck cites, in 1990, the uniform of an admiral in the Serbian navy: the trappings of office in a non-existent state, and a territory with no access to the sea.[52] The symbols serve, argues Franck, 'in cueing a government's entitlement to the full range of rights and privileges that come with peer status'.[53] Clearly, there are practical advantages to be gained from international approval. Describing the assertion of the political and religious identity of James I and VI in Stuart court sermons, Lori Anne Ferrell lists among the selective audience 'privy councillors, court hangers-on, continental observers, university scholars, and British clerics'.[54] The 'continental observers' were not there out of mere theological curiosity. And the changing attitudes of world rulers towards the rulers of South Africa, as David Black and Audie Klotz have argued, first legitimated and then de-legitimated Afrikaner nationalism in a way which had practical consequences.[55] But the other examples of diplomatic and inter-state ritual which Franck gives illustrate forcefully that such rituals cannot be reduced to mere symbols. The rituals and the identities which they cultivate and confirm are themselves an important part of the 'rights and privileges that come with peer status'. And whilst no benefit or good can be depicted in total isolation from any other which a person may enjoy, it is as plausible to describe access to material benefits and services as assisting the cultivation and confirmation of legitimating identity, as vice versa. Franck does not go quite this far, though his argument suggests such a resolution. Recognition, he argues, 'is of great practical significance to the beneficiary – in getting the mail delivered, a loan advanced or repaid, etc. – and may well be guided by such utilitarian considerations. However, these acts of validation have additional symbolic dimension. By using symbolism tactically, they help the new entity consolidate its authority.'[56] But unless 'authority' is to be reduced to a mere means of getting the post

---

52 Franck, *The Power of Legitimacy Among Nations*, pp. 110–11.
53 Ibid., p. 116.
54 Lori Anne Ferrell, *Government by Polemic: James I, the King's Preachers, and the Rhetorics of Conformity, 1603–1625* (Stanford, Stanford University Press, 1998), p. 11.
55 David Black and Audie Klotz, *International Legitimation and Domestic Political Change: Implications for South African Foreign Relations* (Bellville, University of Western Cape, 1995), pp. 1–5.
56 Franck, *The Power of Legitimacy Among Nations*, p. 123. The point is made in a more utilitarian fashion by M. J. Peterson: 'As long as new regimes need recognition, and other

delivered and the loan advanced, it is desirable in itself as the confirmation of sovereign identity.

CONCLUSION

The relation between rulers and the leaders of powerful groups is often represented as either power negotiation, or corruption, or class rule. Recognition by other states has clear financial, military, and political advantages, giving access to organisations which can confer trading, diplomatic, or financial services. But it fulfils another function as well. As Inis Claude comments of the self-presentations of statesmen, 'it is a political judgment by their fellow practitioners of international politics that they primarily seek', above that of either legal opinion or domestic opinion.[57] If the cultivation and confirmation of the authoritative identity of rulers, their legitimation, is conducted to a significant degree in communication with cousins, both internal and external, the approval of those cousins has an importance for rulers which is distinct from any material rewards or sanctions they may have at their disposal. It is a coin which is valued for itself as well, as an important component of the action of ruling. It cultivates and sustains the identities of those involved. It is a mutual exchange of Christmas cards.

governments' recognition decisions are not so predetermined by application of legal rules that they become matters of routine, governments can exploit a new regime's need of recognition for policy ends by withholding recognition unless or until the new regime does certain things', M. J. Peterson, *Recognition of Governments: Legal Doctrine and State Practice, 1815–1995* (Basingstoke, Macmillan, 1997), p. 3.

[57] Claude, Jr, 'Collective Legitimization', pp. 368, 370.

CHAPTER 5

Rebels and vigilantes

It is not only the fortunate with a need to justify their good fortune who legitimate their governing identities. The legitimation of those aspiring to be fortunate is at least as important, and rebels legitimate themselves as vigorously as do rulers. Aspiration is less tangible than achievement, and a conviction of one's own authority can have a relatively greater role in the identity of someone who, waiting on the success of rebellion, lacks armies, palaces, or government offices, and has little more than a belief in their own authority to sustain them. Nor is such legitimation restricted to those rebels who challenge existing government in its entirety by aiming for control of the state. Those vigilantes who seek by coercive direct action against other subjects or citizens to appropriate some of the functions of government by compelling others to act in accordance with their own political, religious, cultural or moral beliefs, will engage in a corresponding legitimation of themselves as the proper exercisers, in a bespoke manner, of governmental power. For rebels and vigilantes alike, self-legitimation, by the cultivation and creation of distinctive identity, is a defining aspect of their political activity. In legitimating themselves in this way, they are defining themselves as set apart from those whom they aspire and claim to lead, govern, or represent.

REBELS ARE NOT NECESSARILY DEMOCRATS

There are normally two contrary aspects to rebellion. On the one hand, a challenge is laid down to the existing regime, and a range of existing values is rejected. But, on the other, the self-legitimation of rebels is likely to be in all manner of ways a mirror image of the legitimation of those whom the rebels seek to overthrow. The credentials of the existing rulers will be challenged or dismissed. But this is unlikely to be solely because they have defaulted on some common contract. They will be rejected as the wrong people, or as occupying positions which rightly belong to others. Writing of the maquis fighting against the German occupation in southern France during the Second World War, H. R. Kedward comments on the way in which the legitimations of the Vichy rulers were appropriated, mirrored, or trumped: 'There were inversions at every turn of the Resistance, and in every act of the maquis. The national and patriotic aim of driving out the occupier, which stood at the forefront of all Resistance motivation, produced more than symbolic inversions of occupation when the maquis "occupied" Oyonnax, Cajarc, Lasalle, and many other villages and small towns, well in advance of the process of liberation.'[1] 'The entire maquis discourse, as a distinctive part of wider Resistance assertion, inverted the notion of legality and proclaimed the rightness and legality of revolt. The Chantieres de la Jeunesse were replaced by the "maquis des jeunes" as the rightful uniformed presence of young men in the countryside';[2] 'The cult of the venerable Pétain as the "Chef" with instinctual charisma, was not just abandoned; it was inverted in the oppositional cult of the maquis *chef*, of the instinctual authority of the young leader for whom many maquisards would, and did, give up their lives.'[3] The members of the resistance developed a counter and combatant patriotism to that of right-wing political and social theorist and propagandist Charles Maurras, whose writings in *L'Action Français* attacked foreigners and outsiders. They depicted instead a broader and more civilised nationalism which included those whom Vichy sought to exclude.[4]

Those who challenge an existing government are likely not simply to reject or dismiss the legitimation claims of existing rulers, but to legitimate themselves with claims drawn from or attuned to the values of their own society, and from the governing legitimations of

---

[1] H. R. Kedward, *In Search of the Maquis: Rural Resistance in Southern France, 1942–1944* (Oxford, Oxford University Press, 1993), p. 283.
[2] Ibid., pp. 283–4.
[3] Ibid., p. 284.
[4] Ibid.

that society. As Dolf Sternberg put it, 'attempts to clothe a usurping power with legitimacy, whether successful or not, have often revealed what the standards of legitimacy are for a given society or civilization'.[5] Communists may challenge the predominant values of capitalism, but not those of democracy, and have frequently used with great success the values of nationalism and patriotism. In democratic societies, or societies where democratic values or aspirations play a major part, legitimation is likely to involve reference to some form of popular sovereignty, just as in societies where rule is legitimated by divine right or human succession, legitimation will be contested in terms of divine sanction or heredity. And what above all rebels normally share, whether their claims are cast in elitist or populist terms, is their attention to the satisfaction of their own sense of authority, in their own eyes. So even if the claim of the rebels is expressed in democratic terms, it can be illuminating to enquire what the function of the democratic argument is, and how it contributes to identifying and legitimating the rebels. Patrick O'Neil argues, of the overthrow of the communist regime in Hungary in 1990, that the revolution 'was the result of a peaceful transition from within and of the Communist party by intellectuals, marginalised after the reform response which followed 1956, but who were finally able to assert themselves in favour of a form of social democracy'.[6] The rhetoric was democratic, but it served to justify the particular position of a new elite, and, paradoxically, to define their distinction from the mass of citizens. Self-description and self-justification thwarted or ignored, was succeeded by self-description and self-justification vindicated.

Nationalist and other revolutionary politics is for these reasons normally best seen as a politics of rebellion rather than of revolution. What is being offered is an alternative government, not an alternative to government. 'It's our country, not theirs',[7] as one nationalist republican put it when talking of Protestants in Northern Ireland, is not necessarily a democratic claim. The activities of

---

[5] Dolf Sternberg, 'Legitimacy' in David L. Sills (ed.), *The International Encyclopedia of the Social Sciences*, vol. IX, pp. 244–8 (New York, Free Press, 1968), p. 244.

[6] Patrick H. O'Neil, 'Revolution from Within: Institutional Analysis, Transitions from Authoritarianism, and the Case of Hungary', *World Politics* 48, 4 (July 1996).

[7] Kevin Toolis, *Rebel Hearts* (London, Picador, 1995), p. 41.

rebels frequently serve to cultivate and confirm their own authority to rule. Each side justified its violence both by giving an account of itself as defender of its community, and by depicting an enemy which threatens that community. The Provisional IRA presented itself as the police force of its community, whilst Protestant violence was justified, particularly in response to the 1985 Anglo-Irish Agreement, on the grounds that its perpetrators were the only true defenders of law and the constitution.[8] Defenders of the constitution, existing or hoped for, are by definition marked off from ordinary subjects and citizens. A member of the Provisional IRA reported that: 'We got a big buzz out of the arms training. I came back with my chest sticking out – "Big Man!" I should have had a sticker printed on my forehead – "TOP MAN NOW!"'[9] It was not only the necessary secrecy of an insurgent terrorist organisation that kept this sticker off the forehead. The knowledge, however humorous, that it could be there, was a satisfaction in its own right, as was the knowledge that one was marked off from the ordinary crowd.

The rhetoric and rituals of nationalism give a central place to the rulers in waiting, the heroes of the nationalist challenge. The most apparently democratic or populist claims can rely on this feature of the politics of rival legitimation. George Orwell, making a case for popular revolution in dialogue with the anti-elitist arguments of American Trotskyism, could nonetheless present the alternatives for Britain in the war years as either Winston Churchill or Stafford Cripps. Even for revolutionary democrats, the choice was not between rulers' power and people's power, but between a leader who was depicted as sharing an identity with the people, and one who was depicted as more closely associated with the old ruling class.[10] The legitimation of rebels by appeals to transcendent principles of religion or morality is essentially similar. For those who conceive of Islam or Christianity or Hinduism as the sole basis for governing authority, the justification is readily available for their own special

---

[8] Alan Bairner, 'The Battlefield of Ideas: the Legitimation of Political Violence in Northern Ireland', *European Journal of Political Research* 14 (1986), 633–49, p. 643.
[9] Quoted in Toolis, *Rebel Hearts*, p. 125.
[10] John Newsinger, 'The American Connection: George Orwell, "Literary Trotskyism" and the New York Intellectuals', *Labour History Review* 64, 1 (1999), 23–43, pp. 27–9.

status, and for the invalidity of the claims of merely secular rulers.[11] Prophets who denounce an entire regime as ungodly, and call for the establishment of government by those who share or apply their own divine insight, are making a claim about themselves at least as sweeping as any they may be making either against existing rulers or for their own religious beliefs. As Hok-lam Chan observes:

The later prophets of Israel could also be considered as performing the function in government that has since come to be called 'the opposition.' In numerous instances, prophecy, based on revelation of a superior will by an extraordinary leader who claimed preconceived knowledge, has also been effective in inspiring volatile political movements, often of a revolutionary nature. It not only sanctioned the leadership of such movements, but also strengthened the legitimacy of the resultant governmental organizations, in the medieval as well as in the modern world.[12]

If the society is one in which rule is conventionally aristocratic or princely, the prince is legitimated by his peculiar insights into the source of the religious sanction. But the use of religion to legitimate single leaders or clusters of leaders can equally be found in societies which make formal acknowledgement of the role of the masses provided there is an employment of other beliefs which have a secure social hold. The Islamist, Sayyid Qutb, writing at the beginning of the 1960s, envisaged a true Muslim prince who would govern according to the law of God, the *shari'a*. Such government would be accomplished by an elite of believers who would, on the one hand, separate themselves from society as it was at present constituted, but on the other, seize control of it in order to inaugurate a godly government.[13] This principle gives an absolute justification to both rulers and rebels. Rebellion is a rejection not of government, but of a government. It does not reject or resist the power of the state, but seeks to appropriate it. And it identifies a select group, marked off by piety, or courage, or insight, or dedication, who are uniquely qualified to undertake

[11] Y. M. Choueiri, 'Theoretical Paradigms of Islamic Movements', *Political Studies* 41, 4 (March 1993); Antony Black, 'Classical Islam and Medieval Europe: A Comparison of Political Philosophies and Cultures', *Political Studies* 41, 1 (March 1993), 58–69.
[12] Hok-lam Chan, *Legitimation in Imperial China: Discussions under the Jurchen-Chin Dynasty [1115–1234]* (London, University of Washington Press, 1984), p. 15.
[13] Quoted by Gilles Kepel, *The Revenge of God: The Resurgence of Islam, Christianity and Judaism in the Modern World* (Cambridge, Polity, 1994), p. 20.

the appropriation. The chosen remnant can be characterised by their religion, or their race, or their class, or their culture, or their political insight, but they will always be characterised in a way which both stresses their exceptional nature, and demonises those against whom, and against whose values, they are opposed.

THE PEOPLE'S REBELLION

It is often assumed or implied that rebels and vigilantes are not an elite, are in fact the very reverse, and that opposition to an existing government or regime will be popular, a movement of the people, an assertion from the bottom of the pyramid of power against the top. Vilfredo Pareto may have cast doubts on this narrative over a hundred years ago with the suggestion that all that ever happened when regimes appeared to be overthrown from below was that one elite replaced another – a circulation of elites. But the democratic values of the twentieth century have sustained a picture of rebellion as offering more than an alternative government, almost an alternative to government. If legitimate government was legitimate because of the support or consent of the people, then challenges to it must, equally, be popular and democratic.

This perspective has been marked in accounts of the most familiar form of popular reaction against existing governments at the close of the twentieth century (both the short twentieth century and the chronological century), nationalism. A widespread assumption in describing nationalism has been that it is a movement of peoples against states, of the led against their leaders, of the many against the few. The national and ethnic groups which constitute the resistance to 'inappropriate' constitutional structures or 'misdrawn' frontiers have been conventionally portrayed as a collective assertion by all the people, or peoples, against a narrow and insufficiently representative political elite, which is in its turn identified with the state, or a ruling class or group. At the very least, nations and ethnic groups are presented as providing the fine tuning for the coarser contours of existing political arrangements, while in less cautious accounts they are depicted as presenting a challenge to the established elites of states such as the United Kingdom. But however they are presented, the assumption, more or less explicit, is that national and ethnic groups are popular, democratic communities, in which the ordinary citizen plays a full and powerful role. Whilst existing arrangements may be elitist, ethnic and national challenges come from the people.

One of the themes running through the writing of a nationalist revolutionary such as Tom Nairn, in books such as *The Break-up of Britain*, *The Enchanted Glass*, or *After Britain*, is just such a division of power and interest. On the one hand, there is the Ukanian 'Crown-State', on the other, the peoples who inhabit the United Kingdom.[14] It is a contrast between popular, if deceived, repressed, side-lined but always potentially triumphant, radical common sense, and elite manipulation which has a strong and varied ancestry. Nairn can quote Chesterton without any substantial irony, and could equally well, had it not threatened to be ideologically disconcerting, have quoted Orwell.[15] The journalist Neal Ascherson spoke in similar terms of the consequences of membership of the European Community for the old systems of governmental power in the United Kingdom: 'Power will escape, flying upwards to the Community – but also downwards to subjects who become citizens, to cities which grow proud and free, to nations like Scotland or Wales which acquire parliaments of their own.'[16] The various proposals that have been mooted for federalism as a solution to the antagonisms of Northern Ireland, for the aspirations of Wales, or for national self-determination for Scotland within the European Community, were approached and discussed principally in terms of the Scots, the Welsh, or the Irish as peoples. A conflict of

---

[14] Tom Nairn, *The Break-Up of Britain: Crisis and Neo-Nationalism* (London, Verso, 1981); Nairn, *The Enchanted Glass: Britain and its Monarchy* (London, Radius, 1988); Nairn, *After Britain: New Labour and the Return of Scotland* (London, Granta, 2000).

[15] The Chesterton quote is the familiar 'We are the people of England, that never have spoken yet', Nairn, *The Break-Up of Britain*, p. 291. Orwell's comment that 'in all societies the common people must live to some extent against the existing order. The genuinely popular culture of England is something that goes on beneath the surface, unofficially and more or less frowned on by the authorities', is in the same tradition. George Orwell, *The Lion and the Unicorn: Socialism and the English Genius* in Orwell, *The Collected Essays, Journalism and Letters of George Orwell*, Sonia Orwell and Ian Angus (eds.), 4 vols. (Harmondsworth, Penguin, 1968), vol. II, p. 78.

[16] Neal Ascherson, 'The Spectre of Popular Sovereignty Looms over Greater England', *The Independent on Sunday*, 18 November 1990, 23.

interests and views was presented not just between governments both existent and hypothetical, but between the existing state and the people, or rather between the existing state and various peoples. Nationalism has been depicted as a popular, even a populist, phenomenon. The state is by contrast presented as an elite, which governs, oppresses, deceives, or holds in artificial uniformity, in defiance of their national or ethnic character, the population at large.

Is this distinction between a state elite and a nationalist people illuminating? Are the legitimation conflicts of nationalism or ethnicity conducted principally, on the nationalist or ethnic side, by or even amongst the masses? Is the national or ethnic claim, even though it may be made on behalf of ordinary people rather than directly by them, nonetheless marked off from the elitism which it challenges not only by national or ethnic distinctiveness, but by a genuine equality in the sharing of power and in the creation, expression, or defence of communal identity? Are those who are portrayed as members of national or ethnic communities, whilst remaining essentially subjects within the existing constitutions or polities which the nationalist claim challenges, truly citizens within those other, alternative communities?

A warning that this might not be so can be deduced from Miroslav Hroch's account of nationalism as having three stages, in each of which it is a nationalist elite which takes the initiative, and indeed during the first two of which ordinary subjects and citizens have no significant part to play at all.[17] National identity is displayed by leaders, who then appeal to ordinary subjects for recognition and support. The nationalist identity, and the legitimation of the nationalist aspiration, always seems clearest, most articulate, in the actions of the minority, most inchoate in the mass. The history of nationalism seems very full of heroes, and charisma lies heavily across the record of national assertion and uprising.

[17] Miroslav Hroch, *Social Preconditions of National Revival in Europe: A Comparative Analysis of the Social Composition of Patriotic Groups among the Smaller European Nations*, trans. Ben Fowkes (Cambridge, Cambridge University Press, 1985); 'From National Movement to the Fully-formed Nation: the Nation-Building Process in Europe', *New Left Review* 198 (March/April 1993), 3–20.

THE ARCHETYPAL REBEL IS A PRETENDER

Treason doth never prosper, what's the reason?
For if it prosper, none dare call it treason[18]

The observation, at the beginning of the seventeenth century,
by Sir John Harington describes an essential similarity between
traitors and monarchs, rebels and rulers. The importance of self-
justification for the rebellious or usurping ruler appears universal.
Charles I was put on trial in the seventeenth century, much as was
Nawaz Sharif in Pakistan in the late twentieth century, as much
to confirm the legitimation of his replacement, as to justify his re-
moval. For if the successful usurper was not a usurper at all, but justified when a rebel, then the ostensible governor was not a justified
governor, and was guilty of usurpation even when he ruled. They
differ only in that one is out and the other is in. The claim can sometimes be grander than any the existing government might make.
When Davide Lazzaretti, the Italian millennial leader, descended
with his followers from the Monte Amiata in 1878, he had already
proclaimed himself as king and Messiah.[19] The archetypal rebel
is a pretender. When the actions of the IRA in Northern Ireland
are described as 'an act of rebellion against what was perceived to
be an illegitimate state',[20] the language of legitimation carries in
its knapsack the claim of an alternative state, and of its aspirant
rulers and leaders. The claim made by the leaders of the Official
IRA at a time when the organisation was sitting on the political
margins, and the military initiative has passed to the Provisional
IRA, to be 'the legitimate government of Ireland'[21] was eccentric,
but it was the eccentric end of a prevalent continuum. The language of heroes and heroism is a frequent feature of the language

[18] Sir John Harington, *Epigrams* (1618), book 4, number 5. The poetic judgement of the
seventeenth century cedes nothing in clarity to the prosaic of the twentieth: 'Revolutions,
unlike usurpations or *coups d'état*, are not necessarily illegitimate. If they succeed they
introduce a new principle of legitimacy that supersedes the legitimacy of the former
regime', Dolf Sternberg, 'Legitimacy', in Sills (ed.), *International Encyclopaedia of the Social
Sciences*, vol. IX, p. 244.
[19] Eric Hobsbawm, *Primitive Rebels*, 3rd. edn (Manchester, Manchester University Press,
1971), p. 69.
[20] Toolis, *Rebel Hearts*, p. 23.
[21] Ibid., p. 316.

of rebellion. The leaders can be more frequently depicted and praised than the people, and the elite of nationalist rebellion aspire to, and are accorded, heroic status. 'Belfast was at war and the IRA was for most Catholics a heroic organization, its Volunteers fêted as the people's defenders.'[22]

The secrecy of nationalism and other forms of rebellion is tactical. But it is not inconsistent with the regnal, or counter-regnal, character of endogenous self-legitimation amongst rebels. The fictional Little Malcolm in David Halliwell's play of the same name,[23] created his leadership self more effectively in the bed-sit than in the street. When rebels speak of 'we' and oppose that ostensibly broad plural to a narrow 'them' what is striking is the narrowness of the 'we' or rather the narrowness of the intense 'we', and the thinness of the broad 'we'. The aspirant nationalist elite is passionate in its internal legitimation.[24] This internalisation is often exacerbated by its rebellious and hence semi-secret manner of operation. It cannot proclaim its beliefs in itself openly, even if it might otherwise wish to do so. So the rebel songs, the Jacobite anthems, have to be sung in secret. This is in part because even those rebel songs which are designed to cultivate public support have to be sung with care. The existing rulers recognise the power of ritual and symbol as weapons in the fight for government. But some of the rituals and representations of rebellion have a limited audience, and are communicated principally or exclusively to the aspirant rulers, whose conception of themselves they serve to mirror. As Hobsbawm put it: 'The classical secret brotherhood was a hierarchical élite group, with a tremendous paraphernalia of initiation and other rituals, symbolism, ritual nomenclature, signs, passwords, oaths and the rest.'[25] At a more exalted level, the royal portraits of the Jacobite court in exile were never glimpsed by the actual or potential supporters of the Stuart claimants to the thrones of England and Scotland. But their imagery was nonetheless carefully constructed to contribute

---

[22] Ibid., p. 105, cf. pp. 110–11, 112, 256.
[23] David Halliwell, *Little Malcolm and his Struggle Against the Eunuchs* (London, Faber, 1967).
[24] As the editor of the *Derry Journal* observed of nationalist rebels such as Martin McGuinness, 'they just seem to feel more intensely about these things than the rest of us', Toolis, *Rebel Hearts* p. 295.
[25] Hobsbawm, *Primitive Rebels*, p. 165.

to the self-legitimation of the Stuarts.[26] For rebels of all kinds, from the Liberty Tree during the War of American Independence to the rituals of Nazism in the 1920s,[27] the internal cohesion of the aspirant state is as important as popular support, and legitimation, or counter-legitimation, is a vital activity for those who see themselves as the rightful exercisers of governmental power. It is a means of cultivating loyalty, identity, and solidarity. Whether or not others believed in them, they needed to believe in themselves. As David Kertzer puts it: 'In order to invest a person with authority over others, there must be an effective means for changing the way other people view that person, as well as for changing the person's conception of his right to impose his will on others.'[28] The second can exist without the first, but the first is ineffective without the second.

THE LEGITIMATION OF REBELS

The self-legitimation of rebels is similar in kind to the self-legitimation of rulers, and is cultivated for the same reasons. As Clifford Geertz comments, 'Thrones may be out of fashion, and pageantry too; but political authority still requires a cultural frame in which to define itself and advance its claims, and so does opposition to it.'[29] Challenging the legitimation of the existing rulers becomes an essential part of the rebellion, because the legitimation of existing rulers denies that of their would-be successors. In Paris in 1871 the communards demolished the Vendôme Column with the statue of Napoleon on it.[30] But that action can be seen not so

---

[26] 'The family portrait painted by Pierre Mignard in 1695 depicts the prince as a bold and majestic youth, standing apart from the trio of his parents and sister: he gestures towards a crown and sword in the foreground of the picture. These two works illustrate the main theme of court art at St. Germain in the 1690s: the hereditary right of the Prince of Wales', Paul Kléber Monod, *Jacobitism and the English People, 1688–1788* (Cambridge, Cambridge University Press, 1989), p. 73.

[27] David L. Kertzer, *Ritual, Politics, and Power* (New Haven and London, Yale University Press, 1988), pp. 162, 166.

[28] Ibid., p. 24.

[29] Clifford Geertz, 'Centres, Kings, and Charisma: Reflections on the Symbolics of Power' in Sean Wilentz (ed.), *Rites of Power: Symbolism, Ritual and Politics Since the Middle Ages* (Philadelphia, University of Pennsylvania Press, 1985), p. 30.

[30] Maurice Agulhon, 'Politics, Images, and Symbols in Post-Revolutionary France', in Wilentz (ed.), *Rites of Power*.

much as a denial of rule, as the cancellation of a visual expression of a claim which clashed with the self-legitimation of the commune.

A group, whether secret or not, which sees itself as entitled to rule, and whose self-description is of an elite with a distinguishing ruling identity, will legitimate itself accordingly. An 'inheritor party' of the kind described by J. P. Nettl in his study of the German Social Democratic Party (SPD) will thus display many of the actions characteristic of rebels, and hence also of rulers: 'By 1911 already the SPD had all the appearance of a state within a state, and when Bebel jocularly referred to the Executive as "your government" no one took exception or expressed surprise at the phrase.'[31] This legitimation by rebels of themselves is part of a broader phenomenon identified by Antonio Gramsci when he described the creation and cultivation of counter-hegemonies by revolutionary movements.[32] To replace one system by another involved replacing one way of depicting the world by another. Legitimation is part of that process of depiction, the depiction of rulers and leaders. Thus when Adam Przeworski discusses the collapse of communist regimes in Eastern Europe in 1989–91, he uses the term counter-hegemony to describe the challenge posed to them by rebellious subjects.[33]

Rebels are not against government. They are more passionately for it than the ordinary citizen or subject. But they believe it is they who are authorised to exercise it. And since they do not exercise it, their legitimation of themselves for the cultivation and maintenance of their own authoritative identity is all the more intense.[34] As Michael Rosen has argued, even to challenge rulers with apparently overwhelming power requires a form of thinking and acting

---

[31] J. P. Nettl, 'The German Social Democratic Party 1890–1914 as a Political Model', *Past and Present* 30 (April 1965), 65–95, p. 78.

[32] Antonio Gramsci, *Selections from the Prison Notebooks of Antonio Gramsci*, ed. and trans. Quintin Hoare and Geoffrey Nowell Smith (London, Lawrence and Wishart, 1971); James Joll, *Gramsci* (London, Fontana/Collins, 1977).

[33] Adam Przeworski, *Democracy and the Market: Political and Economic Reforms in Eastern Europe and Latin America* (Cambridge, Cambridge University Press, 1991), p. 54.

[34] Kevin Toolis's observation and report is relevant. Writing of one IRA man, he observes that he 'wanted what we all probably want – respect from our peers. Ironically, his wife Elizabeth said Paddy told her that if they had been living at peace in a different country he would have wanted to be a policeman', Toolis, *Rebel Hearts*, pp. 204–5. Not perhaps as ironically as all that.

which is beyond the normal perimeters of rational calculations of outcomes.[35] A moral conviction of rightness may be both a requirement and a distinguishing characteristic of successful rebels, but also one which marks them off from the bulk of the population. Rebels thus represent the most acute challenge to the legitimating self-identification of rulers, because they present to government its own mask carried by other players.

So, therefore, far from challenging the activity of government as such, rebels, in legitimating their claims to government, frequently cultivate their own identities in a way which legitimates not simply a different incumbent for the powers of state, but a more extensive and comprehensive use of those powers. The very certainty of the legitimating claim is frequently conducive to a more sweeping ambition for the use of state power.

However populist, nationalist, or democratic the rebels claim may be, there will frequently be a dimension which nonetheless marks the rebels off from the large part of the population. And even if rebels eschew any desire to rule themselves, but describe their aim as catalytic rather than governing, their account of their own catalytic character can have grandiose dimensions. Thus Weatherman, the group within the student radical movement in the United States at the end of the 1960s which advocated terrorism as a means of overthrowing or destabilising capitalism and imperialism, spoke of itself as like the Vandals or Visigoths bringing down the Roman Empire.[36] Political self-effacement could hardly be more flamboyant.

VIGILANTES, LIKE REBELS, LEGITIMATE THEMSELVES

Rebellion presents a comprehensive challenge to an existing regime. But there are too, selective challenges which whilst not seeking to usurp government as such, seek to usurp some of its functions. This is the difference between civil disobedience and dissenting coercion. The former is political and potentially democratic, whereas the latter is an attempt to commandeer some of

[35] Michael Rosen, *On Voluntary Servitude: False Consciousness and the Theory of Ideology* (Cambridge, MA, Harvard University Press, 1996), p. 262.
[36] Harold Jacobs (ed.), *Weatherman* (New York, Ramparts Press, 1970), p. 345.

the functions of rulers. The major symptom of the difference is
legitimation. Engaging in politics does not involve legitimation of
oneself as someone with governing authority: ordinary citizens can
engage in politics. Aspiring to government involves legitimating
oneself as a governor, acting or in waiting. Although those who
seek to exercise the powers of government in respect of particular areas of policy are not challenging the regime or the rulers
in their entirety, they nonetheless legitimate themselves in respect
of the coercive direct action which they undertake. Those who
campaign against abortion in the United States by means of arson
and murder, present themselves in apocalyptic terms as divinely
inspired and authorised, as saints, prophets, and martyrs. 'We, the
remnant of God-fearing men and women of the United States of
Amerika [*sic*], do officially declare war on the entire child killing
industry.'[37] The divine sanction confers and confirms both minority
status and exceptional status, the qualifications of an elite. As such,
the violent opponents of abortion authorise themselves to employ
coercion against their fellow citizens and hence to govern them.
Michael Griffin, who murdered a doctor working at an abortion
clinic, was described by Michael Bray, another prominent activist
in the violent fundamentalist Christian anti-abortion movement,
as having acted 'legally, morally, and heroically'.[38] The law of God
gave members of the direct action anti-abortion organisation Operation Rescue a sanction which could trump their obligation to
earthly laws. Randall Terry of Operation Rescue, who referred to
himself as 'God's anointed', claimed that 'We have an injunction
in the Bible that commands us to rescue innocent children . . . We
fear God, the supreme judge of the world, more than we fear a
federal judge.'[39] 'Christian patriots' of this kind believe themselves
to be the guardians of a culture, a religion, a constitution, and a
race which is under threat from a world-wide conspiracy. They see
themselves as under a sacred obligation to resist a pervasive enemy, though not necessarily on behalf of all people. Some of them

---

[37] 'Army of God' manual, quoted in Jim Risen and Judy Thomas, *Wrath of Angels: The
American Abortion War* (New York, Basic Books, 1997), p. 351.
[38] Risen and Thomas, *Wrath of Angels*, p. 358.
[39] Ibid., pp. 237, 327.

divide humanity into God's humans and Satan's humans, the latter classified not entirely as a result of free will, but by race amongst other identities.[40] The chosen governors, in such a perspective, are not just select, but permanently select.

The legitimating justifications which in the United States went into the campaigns against abortion, in England went into campaigns for animal rights.[41] Arson and various forms of sabotage used by animal rights activists in the United Kingdom can be justified by militants by appeals to 'the higher law of which they are guardians'.[42] A leading member of the Animal Liberation Front can exhort in the language of heroes, 'History is in the making but, so much more importantly, we have evil on the run. Be brave, be strong, be determined.'[43] Vigilantes can frequently be leaders in sheep's clothing. Their language is egalitarian and fraternal rather than elitist. But the language used and the appeals made can nonetheless evoke governing authority, whatever the size of the governing group. Politics could be described as 'toadying to the public',[44] and the hope of achieving change through the politics of persuasion 'an impossible dream'. The way forward was by direct action whereby the '"animals for food trade" will be smashed, destroyed, and finally buried'.[45] In this activity, the activists set themselves apart from the bulk of humankind who were dismissed as 'selfish' or 'scum'.[46] A dismissal of ordinary people is not a necessary aspect of an elevation of one's own self-image, but it can be a powerful obverse. The less seriously ordinary people are assessed, the more remarkable, if only by default, is the actual or potential leadership.

[40] James A. Aho, *The Politics of Righteousness: Idaho Christian Patriotism* (Seattle, University of Washington Press, 1995).
[41] The two countries illustrated reversals of opposition in this case. In the United Kingdom the anti-abortion movement was generally law abiding whilst the animal rights movement used terrorism, in the United States the reverse was the case.
[42] Keith Tester and John Walls, 'The Ideology and Current Activities of the Animal Liberation Front', *Contemporary Politics* 2, 2 (1996), 84.
[43] *Liberator*, Spring/Summer 1995, quoted in ibid., p. 90.
[44] Ronie Lee of the ALF, quoted in David Henshaw, *Animal Warfare: The Story of the Animal Liberation Front* (London, Fontana/Collins, 1989), p. 34.
[45] David Henshaw, *Animal Warfare*, p. 93.
[46] Ibid., pp. 34, 56.

THOSE WHO SEEK TO GOVERN, EITHER IN WHOLE
OR IN PART, LEGITIMATE THEMSELVES

This chapter has neither answered nor addressed an old question in political science, 'Why do people rebel?' Many contributions to the answer to that question, however, have been limited by a merely utilitarian conception of rebellion, as the response to intolerable deprivation.[47] And the answers, in consequence, have sometimes been to another question, 'How or in what manner do people rebel?' Gurr's hypothesis that the 'intensity and scope of normative justifications for political violence vary strongly and inversely with the intensity and scope of regime legitimacy',[48] is a neat instance of this. Separate aspects of a single situation are separated out as explanations of each other, without pursuing the clue thereby provided to a rounder and multidimensional account of rebellion.

The creation and cultivation of authoritative identities is part of the reality or the aspiration of government. To say that one should govern, or that one should exercise some of the powers of government, is to say that one is a particular kind of person, with particular qualities and qualifications, a particular identity. To call yourself the messenger of God, or the father of the nation, or the defender of the weak, is in each case to set yourself apart from ordinary people, whether subjects or citizens. There is an old anarchist joke that whoever you vote for, the government always gets in. It could be said that whoever you support in a rebellion, the government always wins. If legitimation were only for ordinary men and women, then rebels would not need to engage in it. Rebels differ from rioters, protesters, and all other kinds of opponents of rulers in that they believe themselves fitted and entitled to govern in place of the present incumbents. But governing can be a limited activity as with anti-abortion or anti-animal-testing campaigners who seek to regulate one aspect only of their fellow citizens' behaviour. Legitimation may not be the sole litmus test to distinguish rebels from critics, but it is a characterising difference. Revolutionaries

---

[47] Ted Gurr's is the classic exposition of this approach, T. R. Gurr, *Why Men Rebel* (Princeton, Princeton University Press, 1970), but cf. Michael Rosen, *On Voluntary Servitude: False Consciousness and the Theory of Ideology* (Cambridge, MA, Harvard University Press, 1996).
[48] Gurr, *Why Men Rebel*, p. 185.

may be fish who swim in the sea of the people, but the amount
of water they can use is limited both by their own resources and
power, and by the need for secrecy until they are no longer revolutionaries, but rulers. Yet despite this, rebels legitimate themselves to
the full extent of their resources, and they do so because they need
to, not in order to persuade the masses, but to persuade themselves.
One consequence of this is that it can be as difficult for rebels to
surrender as it can be for rulers. For to do so involves a contradiction between their self-description and perception, and others of
their actions. A redescription becomes necessary, and this can be at
least as difficult as an admission of tactical or strategic failure. The
journalist Andrew Marr commented perceptively on an instance
of this difficulty when discussing the demands being made in the
early Spring of 2000 that the IRA in Northern Ireland should begin to give up their weapons. When weapons are given up, wrote
Marr, those who previously used or who had possession of arms
'are the only people who lose. They lose local status, they lose the
grim romance of it all – and now they are told they must lose their
weapons, the tangible emblems of their power and status.'[49] The
conflict of identities which is part of rebellion is so severe that it
cannot easily be resolved save by a change of rulers. But the conflict can arise either from the severity of the difference, or from the
absence of other means of resolving it. Democratic politics provide
a means of reconciliation, or of remedy by replacement, and the
possibilities of this are discussed in chapter 6.

[49] Andrew Marr, 'IRA Must Stop This Idiocy', *The Observer*, 6 February 2000, 26.

CHAPTER 6

Citizens

PRIVATE LEGITIMATION

Rulers legitimate themselves in the sight of their subjects. But though they do so in part to impress their subjects, they do so also in order to impress themselves. The self-legitimation of government, and of governing identity, is an activity which appears to have little regard to the views or approval of the larger part of the population. It is an activity which is more conducive to seeing the mass of people as subjects rather than as citizens. In that respect, endogenous self-legitimation is comparable to other aspects of rule, and to the 'basic confidence to *know* that you're right when everyone else is saying that you're wrong' which is essential to rulers.[1] Rulers are not in the first instance concerned about what those whom they rule think, nor whether their own cultivated image of themselves is recognised and approved of by ordinary people. Indeed they may well deliberately act in a way which excludes their rituals and ceremonies of legitimating identity from public gaze, hearing, or knowledge. The relative indifference to their subjects on the part of rulers corresponds to a relative distribution between rulers and subjects, of the attention given to legitimation. Self-legitimation is a continuous concern of rulers. It is at best an intermittent concern of subjects. The distribution of attention to legitimation corresponds, too, to the distribution of attention to government. Governing is inherently and by definition an undemocratic activity. To rule is to command other people, not to be commanded by them.

---

[1] An anonymous Newcastle local government planner, in J. Gower Davis, *The Evangelistic Bureaucrat* (London, Tavistock, 1972), p. 119, quoted in John Gyford, *Citizens, Consumers, and Councils: Local Government and the Public* (London, Macmillan, 1991), p. 16.

Government is always by somebody, of somebody. It requires both rulers and ruled. Legitimation is undertaken as part of the activity of governing, which is a continuous and absorbing activity; the activity of being governed, despite the extension of the modern state, is not. Legitimation is not a part of normal public life for most people most of the time. So even whilst rulers legitimate themselves in the sight of their subjects, and even though they do so in part to impress their subjects and to cultivate their assent and support, they do so also in order to impress themselves. If one asks, 'where, by whom, and for whom?' is the activity of legitimation carried on, the answer in almost every case will be 'amongst rulers, by rulers, and for rulers'.

PUBLIC LEGITIMATION

However much rulers may legitimate themselves, they engage also in public displays. The fact that the public legitimation of rulers is the most evident to most observers does not make it the most significant for rulers. But it is nonetheless a consistent aspect of the conduct of rulers, and requires explanation. The question 'what are rulers doing in the public rites of legitimation?' has no single or simple answer. It is nonetheless important. Beyond the inner and outer circles of government lies the area of politics which has been the starting point for democratic theorists, and for political scientists whose analytical and descriptive work contains democratic assumptions or aspirations. It is here that legitimation in the sight and in the hearing of the ordinary subjects of government is carried out. The context in which such legitimation takes place is popular: the forum, the street, the newspaper, the cinema, the radio, television, or the internet. The focus of writing and research on such legitimation in the sight and hearing of ordinary subjects is, correspondingly, on the voters, on their stated opinions, their socioeconomic character, on turnout, and on shifts in party support. It is appropriate and unsurprising that the focus of studies of democratic politics is on the demos, rather than on the most persistently active players in the democratic political game.

And yet despite this, the principal actor, the most consistently engaged performer, is still not the subject, but the ruler. Rulers,

governors, politicians not only take the most consistently sustained
role in democratic politics, but they can have an important role in
shaping the character of the human environment within which the
game is played. It has been argued by Patrick Dunleavy in criticism of Anthony Downs that the actions of political parties and of
government can play a significant part in cultivating the aspirations of voters.[2] But rulers can be active in democratic situations
in other ways as well. They can arrange, purchase, coordinate,
require, or summon up displays of recognition of themselves, from
the 'spontaneous' demonstrations of Soviet Russia or Communist
China to the statue erection campaigns orchestrated by the government of Louis XIV.[3] What standard democratic theory can ignore
is that it is rulers, and aspirant rulers, not citizens, who are the
active players. This has always been the argument of elite theorists,
from Weber and Michels to Schumpeter. Schumpeter's fusion of
democratic and elitist theory accorded the active role to leaders
in competing for the support of the electorate for policies which
they supported, but did not generate.[4] George Bernard Shaw presented a more graphic version of the same insight fifty years earlier,
commenting that it was as absurd to expect the voters to be the
source of policies as it was to expect the audience to write the
play.[5]

And whilst one part of the public performances of rulers serves
to cultivate the aspirations and aversions, the loyalty and acquiescence, of subjects, that is not their only role. The parades and
trumpets arranged by rulers have a function which is the very opposite of that normally ascribed to the circuses which ice the bread
dispensed to the people. They may indeed serve to conscript the
loyalties of the populace, but they also provide, on a massive scale,
Christmas cards for the king. The admiration of the crowd is an

[2] Patrick Dunleavy, *Democracy, Bureaucracy and Public Choice: Economic Explanations in Political Science* (Hemel Hempstead, Harvester Wheatsheaf, 1991), pp. 102–4.
[3] Christel Lane, 'Legitimacy and Power in the Soviet Union through Socialist Ritual', *British Journal of Political Science* 14 (1984), 207–17; Christel Lane, *The Rites of Rulers: Ritual in Industrial Society – the Soviet Case* (Cambridge, Cambridge University Press, 1981); Peter Burke, *The Fabrication of Louis XIV* (New Haven, Yale University Press, 1992), p. 96.
[4] Joseph A. Schumpeter, *Capitalism, Socialism, and Democracy*, 5th edn (London, George Allen and Unwin, 1976, 1st edn 1943), pp. 269–83.
[5] George Bernard Shaw, *Ruskin's Politics* (London, Ruskin Centenary Council, 1921), p. 15.

expression of support. It is also identity confirming. A ruler is some-one who does not wish to be an *éminence grise*, with his significance known only to himself. The enjoyment of that identity may in autocracies of one kind or another be largely beyond the public gaze, but if the public is a significant element in the polity, then its role is as a mirror on the wall, telling the ruler that he or she is indeed the fairest of them all. The paradox is that in such self-legitimation, rulers both accord importance to the mass of the people, and deny it, concentrating significance on themselves alone. The paradox is accentuated at the furthest remove from open democratic poli-tics. The satisfaction which the German Führer Adolf Hitler gained from seeing himself as mirrored in the nation is an extreme instance of this: 'I stand here as representative of the German people. And whenever I receive anyone in the Chancellery, it is not the private individual Adolf Hitler who receives him, but the Leader of the German nation – and therefore it is not I who receive him, but Germany through me.'[6] The greater the apparent dependence of the ruler on the mass of ordinary subjects, on whom he claims to depend and of whom he presents himself as no more than a representative, the greater his exceptional character as depicted by himself and for himself becomes, and the greater the gulf between ruler and subjects.

DEMOCRATIC THEORY AND LEGITIMATION

Democratic theories which attempt to make a dynamic connec-tion between normative arguments about legitimacy, and histori-cal accounts and predictions about the behaviour of subjects, might seem to have little interest in, and little to gain from, an account of endogenous self-legitimation as an activity most actively carried out by those within the permanently active centres of power. The principal strands in democratic theories of legitimation are that legitimation is a process whereby voters consent to government,[7]

---

[6] Quoted by Charles Goodsell, *The Social Meaning of Civic Space: Studying Political Authority through Architecture* (Lawrence, University Press of Kansas, 1988), p. 4.

[7] E.g. Jean Blondel, Richard Sinnott, and Palle Svensson, *People and Parliament in the European Union: Participation, Democracy, and Legitimacy* (Oxford, Clarendon Press, 1998); Grainne de Búrca, 'The Quest for Legitimacy in the European Union', *Modern Law Review* 59

or authorise government, or consider government normatively acceptable, or its actions and policies just,[8] or express their wishes in a manner which creates a democratic will which government then expresses.[9] In a version which gives a less active role to voters, a more active one to the outside observer, legitimation is argued to arise from a correspondence of values between rulers and ruled.[10] In each case, government is the activity and rulers are the persons who are legitimated, and the role of citizens is to initiate or authorise the process, rather than to engage in it in any autonomous or self-sufficient way. But whether citizens are seen as clients of government, or are accorded a more active role, legitimation is not a process of which states are simply the objects. At the end of the analysis, legitimation is about rulers, and once the citizens have made their contribution, and that contribution has been assessed, they can be put temporarily to one side of the account. Even if they begin with the status of active subjects in the business of legitimation, it is not a status they continuously retain. If the

(1996), 349–76; Juan J. Linz, 'Legitimacy of Democracy and the Socioeconomic System' in Mattei Dogan (ed.), *Comparing Pluralist Democracies: Strains on Legitimacy* (Boulder, CO, Westview Press, 1988); R. Judson Mitchell, 'Leadership, Legitimacy, and Institutions in Post-Soviet Russia', *Mediterranean Quarterly* 4, 2 (1993), 90–107; Helen Wallace, 'Deepening and Widening: Problems of Legitimacy for the EC' in Soledad Garcia (ed.), *European Identity and the Search for Legitimacy* (London, Pinter, 1993); J. H. H. Weiler, 'After Maastricht: Community Legitimacy in Post-1992 Europe' in Adams (ed.), *Singular Europe: Economy and Polity of the European Community after 1992*, 11–41 (Ann Arbor, University of Michigan Press, 1992); Karlheinz Reif, 'Cultural Convergence and Cultural Diversity as Factors in European Identity' in Soledad Garcia (ed.), *European Identity*.
[8] Tom R. Tyler, 'Justice, Self-interest, and the Legitimacy of Legal and Political Authority' in Jane J. Mansbridge (ed.), *Beyond Self-Interest*, 171–9 (Chicago, University of Chicago Press, 1990).
[9] Seyla Benhabib, 'Towards a Deliberative Model of Democratic Legitimacy' in Seyla Benhabib (ed.), *Democracy and Difference: Contesting the Boundaries of the Political* (Princeton, Princeton University Press, 1996); J. Cohen, 'Deliberation and Democratic Legitimacy' in Alan P. Hamlin and Philip Pettit, *The Good Polity: Normative Analysis of the State* (Oxfords, Blackwell, 1989); John S. Dryzek, *Discursive Democracy: Politics, Policy and Political Science* (New York, Cambridge University Press, 1990).
[10] Peter G. Stillman, 'The Concept of Legitimacy', *Polity* (Amherst, North Eastern Political Science Association) 7, 1 (Fall 1974), 32–56; H. Eckstein, *Support for Regimes: Theories and Tests*, Centre for International Studies, Woodrow Wilson School of Public and International Affairs, Research Monograph 44 (Princeton, Centre for International Studies, 1979). A similar view is part of the argument of David Beetham, *The Legitimation of Power* (London, Macmillan, 1991).

appropriate criteria are met, then government is deemed legitimate.[11] Legitimacy is a quality of states which in some sense have the active consent of their citizens. But the paradox of this account is that it proceeds from democratic premises to a concluding statement which is not about citizens, but about rulers, a judgement and a description not of politics, but of government. The final focus rests on rulers, whose occupation, and the study of whose occupation, is justified in the last resort by the rights and interests of citizens, rather than on those citizens themselves who are the reason for both the practical and the academic exercises.

THE LEGITIMATION OF CITIZENS

Subjects also legitimate themselves, as citizens. They do so most obviously by voting, but also by party and group activities, by demonstrations, strikes, and public campaigns. It has been the central complaint about the account given by Weber of legitimation, that it leaves democracy out of account, or implicitly or explicitly puts it to one side.[12] Certainly Weber was sceptical about democracy and legitimation, but if his arguments are followed further than he took them, a rather different conclusion can be reached. The alternative account developed from the argument in this book presents legitimation, self-confirmation and justification taking place in all sectors of the concentric circles of government. Such an account of endogenous self-legitimation might seem to jar with the prevailing perception of legitimation, or rather of legitimacy, in modern states. What therefore, if anything, is to be said about democracy both as a

[11] Thus one strand of analysis of democratisation sees the process as involving the active consent and involvement of citizens, and describes such a condition either as legitimacy *tout court*, or as conducive to legitimacy. See, for instance, Adam Fagin, 'Democratization in Eastern Europe: The Limitations of the Existing Transition Literature', *Contemporary Politics* 4, 2 (June 1998), 147: 'the formal democratic institutions and mechanisms now established may lack the capacity to effectively channel a diversity of societal interests and, without any foundation within society, will not deliver inclusiveness and legitimacy'.

[12] Dolf Sternberg, 'Typologie de la Légitimité' in P. Bastin *et al.*, *L'Idée de Légitimité* (Paris, Presse Universitaire de France, 1967), p. 96; David Beetham, *Max Weber and the Theory of Modern Politics* (London, 1974), p. 266; Rodney Barker, *Political Legitimacy and the State* (Oxford, Clarendon, 1990), pp. 52–4.

political practice and as a political value, in the light of the description of legitimation as the self-justifying, self-identifying activity of rulers? What is going on, not normatively but historically in 'democratic legitimation'? When this question has been answered, a different account of democratic politics is available. Available democratic approaches to the matter of legitimation may give a misleading account of the actual distribution of energies, and both underestimate, ignore, or dismiss the self- legitimation of rulers. But they may also not pay sufficient attention to the self-legitimation of citizens.

If legitimation is an activity which serves to confirm the identity of the legitimator, then democratic legitimation is not an exception to this function. In so far as people act as citizens as well as subjects, they too engage in actions, legitimations which cultivate, sustain, create, or confirm that identity. 'Democratic legitimation' is most commonly thought of as the transfer of consent from citizens to government. But there is another activity, also democratic, also legitimation, whereby subjects cultivate and sustain their own identity, the legitimation, not of rulers, but of citizens. Democracy involves subjects cultivating their own identity as participating and active members of a polity. A recognition of the self-legitimation of rulers, in other words, is only problematic for democrats if it is not realised that citizens too legitimate themselves, and do so in a way which makes them more than simply clients of a democratically sanctioned state. So it is appropriate to ask where this activity can be observed. What do subjects do which seems to have a function for them similar to that of the various self-legitimating actions conducted by rulers?

To begin by asking what actions subjects take which identify them not just as subjects, but as citizens, is to draw immediate attention to the characterising feature of democracy in modern states: voting. A great deal of attention has been devoted to voting, but much or most of it casts little light on this question. For normative theorists, voting is the exercise of choice or the granting of consent. For explanatory or descriptive political scientists, particularly those using variants of rational choice theory, voting is a calculated investment of time and energy. Drawing attention to the adequacies and inadequacies of the second of these bodies of work,

Donald Green and Ian Shapiro have argued for more attention to be paid to the phenomena, less to the method.[13] An account of voting in terms of rationally appraised costs and benefits, they suggest, has to rely to a disconcerting extent on the value to voters of 'psychic gratification'.[14] But this entails asking what exactly are people doing when they vote in elections for representative assemblies. Responding to such criticisms, Stewart Wood and Iain McLean make the significant observation that the attack on rational choice theory and voting is justified, and that while it 'makes little sense to argue that voters are rational calculators, it makes a lot of sense to argue that legislators and lobbyists are'.[15] But the limitations of the usefulness of rational choice theory arise not from an ignoring of non-rational forms of action, but from an inadequate conception of the individual or the self who makes the rational calculations in the first place. The listing by William Riker and Peter Ordeshook of 'psychic gratifications' which might be fed into a rational balancing of the costs and benefits of voting, includes 'complying with the ethic of voting', 'affirming a partisan preference', and 'affirming one's efficacy in the political system'.[16] Two things are notable about this listing. The first is that 'complying with the ethic of voting' is strikingly reminiscent of Weber's sense of duty. Acting in a particular way because it is consistent with an ethic or value is what Weber was describing when he spoke of the bureaucrat fulfilling the obligations of his office because not to do so would be 'abhorrent to his sense of duty'.[17] The second is that each of the three gratifications cited is a form of identity cultivation, assertion, and maintenance. If the individual is seen as someone who actively asserts, maintains, and cultivates his or her identity, actions such as

[13] Donald P. Green and Ian Shapiro, *Pathologies of Rational Choice Theory: A Critique of Applications in Rational Choice Theory* (New Haven, Yale University Press, 1994), p. 203. Green and Shapiro argue for a more eclectic use of theory, and accounts which pay attention both to rational and other aspects of political action.

[14] Ibid., p. 49.

[15] Stewart Wood and Iain McLean, 'Recent Work in Game Theory and Coalition Theory', *Political Studies*, 43, 4 (December 1995), 703–17, p. 706.

[16] William Riker and Peter C. Ordeshook, *Introduction to Positive Political Theory* (Englewood Cliffs, NJ, Prentice Hall, 1973), p. 63, quoted in Green and Shapiro, *Pathologies of Rational Choice Theory*, p. 51.

[17] Max Weber, *Economy and Society*, Guenther Roth and Claus Wittich (eds.), 2 vols. (London, University of California Press, 1978), p. 31.

voting no longer lie outside a world of rationally acting individuals. Green and Shapiro provide a clue in this direction when they comment that one of the reasons for the unfruitfulness of rational choice theory when applied to voter turnout is that such theories are 'silent about the process by which people develop tastes and identities'.[18] The problem here is not the irrationality of voting, but the inadequate conception of rationality, which takes identities and interests as given, rather than as dynamic, and which fails to take account of identity cultivation, maintenance, and expression, as a major part of public life.

An analysis of voting as a rational investment of time and effort in the pursuit of tangible utility can cast light on marginal variations in voting, on the level of turnout, the extent of abstention, or changes in party allegiance. It has less to say about the initial action of voting as such, since this involves forms of political action which fall outside, or prior to, rational action as conventionally conceived.[19] Voting is a self-legitimating activity for citizens. Questions about how people apportion their votes, about the numbers who vote, about changes in allegiance, are all auxiliary to the primary question of why people vote at all. That question is best answered if it is replaced by another: 'what are people doing when they vote?' This is the question which arises from Green and Shapiro's recommendation that more attention be paid to phenomena, less to method, that political science in other words be properly empirical and historical, and less deductive.

In so far as voting is part of the cultivation of identity, voters are clearly doing something different from rulers. Although democracy can be described as government by the people, voters are not governing. At the very strongest, they are choosing governors. But that is an action of identity legitimation. In voting, citizens are acting out, creating, sustaining, and legitimating their character as significant members of political society. They are demonstrating and enacting, particularly to themselves, their character as arbiters of the composition of governments, or legislative assemblies, or

---

[18] Green and Shapiro, *Pathologies of Rational Choice Theory*, p. 68.
[19] Kay Lehman Schlozman, Sidney Verba, and Henry E. Brady, 'Participation's Not a Paradox: The View from American Activists', *British Journal of Political Science*, 25, 1 (January 1995).

public officers. So an extension of the legal right to vote, such as that in Britain in 1867, can be described as 'a critical moment in the construction of a new "rational and respectable" male political subject'.[20] Rulers legitimate themselves. So do citizens, and in so doing they often challenge the confidence of ruling elites. Hence the outrage amongst those whose self-reflected identity is that of members, or close cousins, of a ruling elite at the *presumption* of the rituals and language of citizenship. Despite the fact that even in democracies the citizens only impinge on the activity of ruling sporadically, whereas full-time rulers rule full time, the people, even though with less intensity and far less regularity or continuity, legitimate themselves. In a democracy they legitimate themselves as citizens.

To legitimate is to authorise or justify by confirming identity. There are other ways of doing this than voting, which complement the ballot. And just as it has been argued that voting is an insufficient exercise of citizens' power and that, for instance, strikes are a far more effective means of political action,[21] or that the English as typical democrats by representation are free only once every five years, so it can be argued that voting is only one of the ways in which citizenship identity is expressed and cultivated. When people demonstrate or petition, march or protest, deface or destroy the symbols of government, they are asserting or creating their own identity, and legitimating themselves. The actions of democratic demonstrators in Poland in the years leading up to the revolution of 1989 were not only a pressure applied to the regime, they were also an expression, cultivation, and confirmation of the people as citizens. The people were legitimating themselves as the *demos*, and the banners and symbols, both secular and religious, of the demonstrations were an expression and a creation of the citizen identity of the protestors.[22] The way in which the people legitimate their political identities will often be a deliberate reversal of the legitimation

[20] James Vernon (ed.), *Re-reading the Constitution: New Narratives in the Political History of England's Long Nineteenth Century* (Cambridge, Cambridge University Press, 1996), p. 11.

[21] R. A. Leeson, *Strike: A Live History 1887–1971* (London, George Allen & Unwin, 1973), p. 13.

[22] Jan Kubik, *The Power of Symbols against the Symbols of Power: The Rise of Solidarity and the Fall of State Socialism in Poland* (Pennsylvania, Pennsylvania State University Press, 1994).

of rulers, using, and inverting, the symbols and claims of those they oppose in order to express their own identity, grievances, or claims. When demonstrators marched to Dublin Castle in 1897 on the occasion of Queen Victoria's Silver Jubilee, they used the event of the Jubilee celebrations, but marked it with their own rituals and symbols: a draped coffin, a banner reading 'Starved to Death'.[23] The rituals of popular procession can rival in their symbolic elaborateness the ceremonies of established authority. Trade union banners in Britain in the nineteenth and twentieth centuries were woven, embroidered and painted celebrations of the identity of those who carried and followed them, and were a rich obverse version of the religious and secular imagery of governing authority.[24] The antagonistic identifications of Northern Ireland in the late twentieth century were similarly cultivated in paraded banners and regalia.[25]

When citizens legitimate themselves, they strengthen themselves. They cultivate, sustain, and develop both their role as powerful foundation members of the polity, and their claim that their views both formally expressed in the ballot and informally expressed in demonstrations, meetings, agitations, and protests should as a matter of course be heeded by their rulers. Seen in this light, the discussion of self-legitimation, whether of rulers or of citizens, may appear less distant from some at least of the democratic concerns of normative political theorists, and of those who have sought to construct theories with both normative and historical/empirical dimensions.

LEGITIMATION, IDENTITY, AND THE STABILITY OF GOVERNMENT

The account I have given is not inconsistent with a democratic political science, or with its democratic normative aspirations.

---

[23] E. Hammerton and D. M. Cannadine, 'Conflict and Consensus on a Ceremonial Occasion: The Diamond Jubilee in Cambridge in 1897', *Historical Journal* 24 (1981), p. 113.

[24] John Gorman, *Banner Bright* (Harmondsworth, Allen Lane, 1973).

[25] Dominic Bryan, *Orange Parades: The Politics of Ritual, Tradition and Control* (London, Pluto, 2000).

Neither the self-legitimation of rulers in the sight of subjects, nor the self-legitimation of subjects, appears to be accounted for in standard democratic theory. There is at first sight an antagonism between the two different perspectives. In one case the democratic argument appears to be undermined by an account of government as the self-referential preoccupation of a ruling elite. In the other case both consent and representation appear to be ignored by an account of citizens as legitimating their identities in a self-referential manner which does not obviously or immediately connect with government. Are we then left with either the unempirical and unhistorical moral or the atheoretical, positivist and amoral, with no possibility of communication between them? I do not believe so. An account of legitimation as an activity of subjects gives more help to democratic theory than this. It suggests how democracy may operate in a distinctive manner to make more likely a correspondence between the self-identification of rulers and ruled, and to make dissonance less likely. And since the self-identification of citizens includes a characterisation and cultivation of them as agents with interests, the avoidance of legitimation dissonance involves coherence of a broad sweep.

THE RELATION BETWEEN LEGITIMATION AND OTHER DIMENSIONS OF POLITICAL ACTIVITY

Before that possibility is examined further, some clarification will be useful of the relations between the self-legitimation of rulers and stable government, and between the legitimating identification of citizens and civic order. If legitimation is taken to be characteristic of all government, and one of its defining features, then it may be thought that it functions in part to make government possible. But it may be that the causal question is misarranged. Just as rulers need to legitimate their identities, to legitimate themselves by identification as rulers in order to rule, so subjects need to legitimate themselves as subjects and hence by inference rulers as rulers, *in order* that they can obey – they do not obey because rulers have been legitimated. Something of this is contained in Michael Rosen's argument about the relation between ideology and compliance, and the role of belief in sustaining or facilitating subordination. 'Non-rational beliefs should be approached, in my view, not as something wholly *pathological* – a deviation from reasonable processes for the formation of consciousness – but as attempts to make the world acceptable by making it intelligible.'[26] For 'intelligible' one might substitute 'coherent' or 'consistent', although the point is similar. We expect actions to be justified. What does that mean? We expect an action to contain as a dimension (dimension rather than aspect, since aspect may be a part, but dimension is a quality of the whole) a claim about its appropriateness. That appropriateness will arise from the character of the actor, and that character will be expressed in action. Compliance with commands is an action, and possesses as a dimension of itself a statement of justification. We do not comply *because* we legitimate compliance. But we cannot readily comply *unless* we legitimate compliance, because legitimation is a dimension of compliance. It does not precede it. Legitimation and identification are then viewed not as a cause or support of obedience, let alone of the securing of obedience, but as a facilitating dimension of it. The understanding of legitimation as the cultivation of coherent character contributes to an understanding of what is happening when people obey, or resist, laws. It explains criminal investigations in a way the prisoner's dilemma cannot. If a criminal decides not to inform on the colleague in the other cell, this may well be for reasons similar to those which motivate Weber's bureaucrat: grassing up associates is not something that people like you do. It is a weakness of rational choice theory that, faced with the existence of legitimation, it tries to describe it as rational support based on a calculation of interest. But whilst that can account for a choice of supermarket, it fits uncomfortably with legitimated government and subordination. More recently, those who have tried to apply the rational individualism of methodological individualism and rational choice theory to government rather than to subjects have seen ideology – of which legitimation becomes a sub-category – as a non-rational alternative or additional explanation for conduct. Both Douglass C. North and, drawing on his work, Margaret Levi, see a belief in the rightness of compliance

[26] Michael Rosen, *On Voluntary Servitude: False Consciousness and the Theory of Ideology* (Cambridge, MA, Harvard University Press, 1996), p. 272.

as a distinct motive, separate from rational compliance, for obeying government.[27]

When people identify a person or group of persons as like themselves they are seeing an idealised or at least improved version of themselves. They see themselves, or values or characteristics which they mark out as characterising themselves, expressed with dramatic grandeur, heightened clarity or colour. The leader or command giver may or may not 'recognise' them in speeches, television appearances, or writing. When we identify with something outside of ourselves, we both recognise it and seek recognition from it. There is an active relation, not simply a passive, observed correspondence.[28] But that recognition is not necessary for them to see in the leader or ruler an idealised, or for the first time truly expressed, expression of themselves. This importance of identity in legitimating rule is well recognised by conservatives. Roger Scruton, comparing monarchs with elected presidential heads of state, comments 'the president will be chosen for his "style", where style carries an implication of inward identity between president and nation'.[29] Those who are most successful in governing, or in challenging government, are those who create, adapt, or present the identity of the political community in a way which most effectively sustains their own legitimation and identification. In this process, the prize goes to those who with greatest skill craft identities, not to those who discover or represent them.[30] When this identification

---

[27] Douglass C. North, *Structure and Change in Economic History* (New York, 1981), ch. 5; Margaret Levi, *Of Rule and Revenue* (London, 1988).

[28] 'Recognition' is a term which has been used in several ways, frequently with a distinctive Hegelian gloss. See, for instance, Charles Taylor, *Multiculturalism and 'The Politics of Recognition'* ed. and introduced Amy Gutmann (Princeton, Princeton University Press, 1992). In the hands of Francis Fukuyama, and ennobled as 'thymos', it is given a crucial role in moving towards the end of history, Francis Fukuyama, *The End of History and the Last Man* (London, Hamish Hamilton, 1992).

[29] Roger Scruton, *The Meaning of Conservatism* (Harmondsworth, Penguin, 1980), p. 39.

[30] Cf. Taylor, *Multiculturalism: Examining The Politics of Recognition*, ed. Amy Gutman, 2nd edn (Princeton, Princeton University Press, 1994). I am doing something much less ambitious than Taylor and his colleagues and critics. They are attempting to set down guidelines for polities; I am trying to give an account which illuminates how polities and their members and subjects relate to one another in the process of legitimation and identification.

can be made, much can be done by the ruler that could not otherwise have been done, much excused, which under a different set of governors would have been inexcusable. Margaret Thatcher, notoriously, asked of a senior civil servant being considered for promotion whether he was 'one of us'.[31] But the relationship worked even more powerfully from the people upwards, and for those for whom Mrs Thatcher was one of them, the character of the leadership carried a force quite distinct from any judgement about the quality of the policies.

Congruence and affinity between legitimations identifies people not policies. A stable relationship between the legitimation and identification of citizens and the legitimation and identification of rulers is a feature of working democracies, where people are able to feel an identification between their own expressed selves and those of their rulers. If subjects feel that their interests as experienced in their own self-identification are not being promoted or defended, the form that dissatisfaction takes will be a contrast between the character of the rulers and their own character as citizens. The complaint will not be that rulers manage the economy incompetently, but that they are incompetent; not that rulers promote the interests of only one party, but that they are partisan; not that rulers fail to defend the interests of the nation, but that they are not patriotic. Hence when politicians or regimes are criticised following a breach of democratic procedures, the most common accusation is not that they have cheated, but that they are cheats. Their breach of procedure, in others words, is not what unfits them, but it has revealed those character flaws which do disqualify them from office. The distinction is important, and explains, for instance, why right-wing governments can be more successful at doing radical things than are left-wing ones, and vice versa. The crucial factor in determining a coherent relationship of legitimations is not the relation between the actions or policies of government and the self-assessed interests of its supporters, but the relation between their conception of themselves – as conservatives, or patriots, or godly, or ordinary working people – and their conception of their rulers. It is no accident that despots are

---

[31] The attributed phrase is used by Hugo Young as the title of his biography, Hugo Young, *One of Us: A Biography of Margaret Thatcher* (London, Macmillan, 1989).

sometimes referred to as the fathers, or mothers, of their people, but not usually as their top managers. Parents share an identity with us that line managers do not. This identification is powerful even when the relationship between subjects and rulers is deferential. For the recognition of superiority occurs within a culture which is seen as distinct from other national cultures. Leaders may exhibit extraordinary qualities, but they are an extraordinary version of qualities which mark us off from our neighbours or our enemies. The power of nationalism lies in evoking a familial identity, which marks us off from other nations who are neither us nor ours.

LEGITIMATION AND UNSTABLE RULE

The legitimation of rulers and that of citizens may not relate to one another. Government is still possible when that happens, but so is coup, rebellion, or abdication. Correspondence or lack of evident conflict between the self-legitimation of rulers and ruled is not necessary, but does make government both more stable and more representative. In the absence or weakness of such correspondence, government is still possible, and subjects whilst they are most likely to be merely acquiescent may still obey the laws and commands of rulers. Walker Connor argues that 'In general, people can pursue their daily business, obey the laws, go to work, and the like, while living in a state to which they do not accord legitimacy.'[32] Jan Pakulski has described Eastern European governments such as that of Poland before 1989 as ruling without the need for any legitimating participation from, or relationship with, their subjects.[33] Michael Rosen has argued that legitimation and ideology have far less to do with explaining the compliance of subjects than is often supposed.[34] It may even be the case that an absence of any correspondence between the self-identification of

[32] Walker Connor, 'Nationalism and Political Legitimacy', *Canadian Review of Studies in Nationalism* 8, 2 (1981), 201–28, p. 217. For a similar argument see Alan James, *Sovereign Statehood: The Basis of International Society* (London, Allen and Unwin, 1986).
[33] Jan Pakulski, 'Poland: Ideology, Legitimacy and Political Domination' in Nicholas Abercrombie, Stephen Hill, and Bryan S. Turner (eds.), *Dominant Ideologies* (London, Unwin Hyman, 1990).
[34] Rosen, *On Voluntary Servitude*, pp. 261–2.

subjects and the perceived identification of rulers can be accompanied by punctilious observance of the law. Religious sects such as Jehovah's Witnesses, Christadelphians, or the Exclusive Brethren, whilst not accepting that the state has any legitimate claim on them, nonetheless scrupulously observe its laws.[35]

The self-identification of subjects and citizens in governing relations other than with conventional states shares many of the same consequences as those more conventionally ruled. An international political organisation such as the Communist Party, a governmental one such as the European Union, or a religious one such as the Roman Catholic Church will exhibit in the relation between the perceived legitimating identities of command givers, and the self-legitimations of ordinary members, features similar to those to be found in the relations between citizens and the rulers of states. Where commands are issued by officials who are members not of state elites but of organisations which either cross state boundaries or claim the allegiance of a part only of a state's subjects, the attitude of those receiving the command will be affected to a major degree by the extent of correspondence between the potential subjects' legitimation and self-identification, and the transmitted legitimation and self-identification of the issuer of the command. Thus a moral instruction from the Papacy may be seen as coming from a unique office in a homogeneous community, or from a distant and cloistered Italian bureaucracy with little association or affinity with the community of the command receiver. The degree of correspondence does not depend on the degree of similarity between the command issuer and a conventional state. Similarly with commands perceived as issuing from the European Commission, or the European Courts of Justice or Human Rights, a major element in their reception is the conception of the degree of correspondence between the legitimated identity of the command issuer, and that of the command receiver.

Whilst pragmatic acquiescence as one possible relation between subjects and rulers does not of itself threaten rulers, citizen

---

[35] Bryan Wilson, 'Religion and the Secular State' in S. J. D. Green and R. C. Whiting (eds.), *The Boundaries of the State in Modern Britain* (Cambridge, Cambridge University Press, 1996): 'Nor, in a country where voting is not compulsory, do these self-imposed restraints lead to direct confrontation with the law, even though, implicitly, they impugn its legitimacy', p. 333.

self-identification does not necessarily sustain them. A move from acquiescence or unenthusiastic obedience to citizen identification is not necessarily a move from indifference to rulers to enthusiasm for them. Much of the growing body of writing on the potential politics of the European Union assumes that the development of a European-wide sense of citizenship, of active membership of a European demos, will legitimate European government, or would even to all intents and purposes be synonymous with such legitimation.[36] That is not necessarily the case. Citizen identification is in the first place the self-identification of citizens, and can be a ground for affinity or dissonance with the self-legitimation of rulers. 'Citizen' is, after all, a word with revolutionary associations as well as participatory ones.

If citizens do not identify with the governed community, they may move to secession or nationalism.[37] If they do not identify with rulers, they may become rebels and seek a form of government which can relate to their own self-identification.[38] In so doing they will undermine the self-legitimation of rulers, increase rulers' lack of confidence, and increase the likelihood of abdication. Rebellion and democratic dissonance are thus significantly different degrees of failed relations between rulers' and citizens' legitimations and identifications. The first is a claim to govern, the second a claim to politics. Rebels are identifying themselves as rulers, dissidents as citizens. In real situations, these distinctions can frequently disappear, but they retain their useful analytical distinctiveness. One of the most frequent ways in which citizens may experience a dissonance between their own legitimated identity and that of their rulers occurs when there is a mismatch of polities, when the polity or governed community which is claimed by the rulers differs from

[36] Reif, 'Cultural Convergence and Cultural Diversity', in Garcia (ed.), *European Identity and the Search for Legitimacy*; Brigid Laffan, 'The Politics of Identity and Political Order in Europe', *Journal of Common Market Studies* 34, 1 (March 1996), 81–103; Heidrun Abromeit, *Democracy in Europe: Legitimising Politics in a Non-State Polity* (Oxford, Berghahn Books, 1998); Dimitris N. Chryssochoou, *Democracy in the European Union* (London, Tauris Academic Studies, 1998).
[37] 'The doctrine that a people ought not to be ruled by those they deemed aliens has rapidly gained converts during the past two centuries', Connor, 'Nationalism and Political Legitimacy', p. 203.
[38] James, *Sovereign Statehood*.

that claimed by citizens. The normal form of this mismatch is a greater claim by rulers, a claim which appears to citizens to be subordinating or homogenising them in a way which challenges or ignores their own legitimating self-identification. So in 1989 when a Conservative government with a British majority, but only minority support in Scotland, introduced the poll tax in Scotland, and did so a year earlier than in England and Wales, this was seen as in part an alien imposition, an affront equally to nationalism and democracy.[39]

Nor of course are rulers simply passive parties to this process. They may respond to dissonance not by amending their own ways, but by amending the character of the governed community. 'Ethnic cleansing' is the most brutal and murderous form of this response, but there are many milder versions. Dissonance between the character of a local government area as expressed in its representatives and the character of its services can lead either to citizens seeking changes because they perceive a clash between their identity and that of local government, or local government seeking to preserve or create a particular social character in the area for which it is responsible. In Southwark from the 1950s onwards it was demands of new arrivals, gentrifiers, ethnic minorities, single parents on a council whose image was nuclear family white working class. In Tower Hamlets in the 1970s it was a council trying to preserve a working-class character, and in Bromley a middle-class character.[40]

DEMOCRACY AND LEGITIMATION

Democracy as rule, or citizen action, by the people solves, or makes less likely, problems of dissonance and is an expression of a condition of things where it is less likely to arise. It provides mechanisms for making coherence more likely. Democracy can be viewed not only as a system of popular government, but as a system of popular restraint on government. In such a view the people do not rule, but they provide a context within which ruling takes place. Applying the account of legitimation in the preceding pages to this view,

[39] Rodney Barker, 'Legitimacy in the United Kingdom: Scotland and the Poll Tax', *British Journal of Political Science* 22, 4 (October 1992).
[40] Gyford, *Citizens, Consumers, and Councils*, pp. 3–4.

it is possible to ask what context, what restraints, are placed on rulers' self-legitimation by the operations of democracy and what associations this has with other aspects of government?

Rulers do not need subjects, or citizens, to enable them to legitimate themselves or to cultivate their governing identities. Their first mirror is themselves, and subjects are at the edge of the outer circle. So what comfort is there for democrats? The actions of citizens will be taken into account in so far as they constrain rulers, and in a democracy electoral defeat is such a constraint. Democracy provides the best available circumstances for securing correspondence between the identification of citizens and the legitimating self-identifications of rulers. The more citizen identity is cultivated, the more there is a possibility of dissonance between the legitimating identification of rulers and the identifications of citizens. The more subjects legitimate themselves as citizens, the greater the significance of that identification for them, and the greater the dissonance if it jars with the legitimated identification of rulers. There are many forms which comparison of the self-legitimating identities of citizens and the expressed self-legitimation of rulers can take, but democracy is the most effective method. Some movements which argue for greater accord between the values of subjects and the values of rulers condemn democracy as 'alien', as has the political movement of puritanical or fundamentalist Islam in Algeria. Democracy, however, involves not only the regular expression of some sort of political opinions by subjects, but regular and free public discussion about the claims of the government and the character of the constitution.[41] In democracies, because there are mechanisms for reducing incoherence, it is less likely to arise. When it does arise, it is likely to do so because there is a lack of coherence between the legitimating identities of citizens and the perceived legitimating identification of rulers. Democratic rules have enabled the voters to detect a discrepancy between their, the electors' view of themselves or at least of their higher selves, and the experienced character of their rulers.

[41] The conformity between constitutional rules and 'shared beliefs' which David Beetham presents as one of his components of legitimacy thus requires democracy not so much for its existence as for its identification. This is distinct from the declaratory and contractual function which Beetham accords such devices as elections, Beetham, *The Legitimation of Power*, pp. 17ff.

I shall argue that it is possible to deploy a workable, if not perfect, theory of legitimation which will be helpful to supporters of democracy. Democracy, or at least some of the values and features associated with it, provides the best hope for an account of legitimation which is both empirically sustainable, and morally acceptable. I shall generalise freely about the politics of legitimation, but do so on the basis of observable rather than ideal conduct. Going with the grain of human experience is only amoral to those who have a non-human standard for humanity.

Democracy is effective not because of any contractarian or popular sovereignty theory, but because elections are a means whereby subjects can choose people they consider to be like themselves. What I am arguing for is therefore not a theory of democracy as the quantification of consent or the aggregation of individual sovereignties.[42] It might seem unremarkable to make such claims for democracy, but it has been more common in fact to argue or assume either that democracy is not a form of legitimacy, or that it is not even a means to legitimacy. Max Weber is the most prominent example of this position, and the example which has been subjected to most criticism. But the North American school contains many similar examples. Parsons's argument about power and legitimacy is at the very least a-democratic, whilst Lipset's is quite specifically elitist and conservative.[43]

If democracy is a context within which rulers operate, the more they do so in the public eye, the more democratic the system. Openness is thus a feature of an ideal democracy not only because it

---

[42] This has been the argument underlying the work on legitimacy of scholars, such as Ted Gurr who speaks of the intensity and extent of legitimacy, the former being 'the extent to which the political unit, its governing institutions, and the incumbents are thought proper and worthy of support', the latter being 'the proportion of people in the political unit with feelings of legitimacy above some specified threshold'. Intensity could be a concept which provided means of distinguishing both between different forms of legitimacy – a qualitative distinction, in other words, arising out of a quantitative one – and of discussing its differential distribution. But in Gurr's use of the term, it is taken to be characteristic of the 'political unit' as a whole, rather than spread within it in, at least potentially, a manner neither even nor uniform, just as power could be in the pluralist model of policy making. Extent, as is proper for a democratic theory, is a matter simply of number, Ted Gurr, *Why Men Rebel* (Princeton, 1970), p. 186.

[43] Anthony Giddens, '"Power" in the Recent Writings of Talcott Parsons'. *Sociology*, 2, 3 (1968), 257–72. Rodney Barker, *Political Legitimacy and the State* (Oxford, Clarendon, 1990), pp. 74–8.

allows citizens the fullest possible information with which to discuss policy, but also because it places the greatest possible restraints on the secret garden of rulers' legitimation, with its potential for losing, or failing ever to establish, connections or affinities with the identifications of citizens.

But even a vigorous and effective democracy does not guarantee a coherence of legitimating identities. There will be sections of ruling groups who are more or less insulated from democratic comparison. And since legitimating identities will always be cultivated in relation to other ruling actions, a lack of coherence between legitimating identities will facilitate a lack of coherence between other actions of rulers on the one hand, and the expressed identities, aspirations, and aversions of subjects on the other.

Because rulers nonetheless seek coherence, there will be continuous contrary pull towards making the public displays coherent with the more private self-legitimation. The image of the duplicitous ruler, whilst it can be sustained by plenty of instances of rulers employing deception and secrecy, cannot so easily be sustained in the manner of legitimating identities. But provided there is no pressure to tailor or shape public displays to make them consonant with the identities of subjects, the possibility of tension or incoherence in the self-legitimation of rulers is insulated against. The principal function of legitimation is to justify rulers in their own eyes. Whilst this appears to be a necessary function of legitimation, it can conflict with the cultivation of legitimate relations between governers and governed if it involves a style or ritual with which the mass of subjects cannot associate themselves. At the extreme end of the spectrum, the legitimation of the ruling groups can become a form of alien triumphalism which decreases and undermines relations of rule and compliance between rulers and ruled. This is particularly the case with imperial or colonial regimes. The very rituals which satisfy and sustain the rulers incite disaffection amongst the ruled.

The necessities of democratic politics provide checks and sanctions against this form of alienation. Democratic elitism, in other words, does not give elites a free hand in determining how they will present themselves either to the electorate or in the face of the electorate. Ian McAllister is thus able to argue, on the basis of a study on citizens and elected representatives in Australia, that 'among legislators, contact with democratic institutions increases support for ethical standards'.[44]

The relationship between democratic politics and greater coherence is organic rather than causal, each sustaining the other and each being aspects of a total complex of actions and patterns of actions which, collectively and in interaction with each other, they constitute. No one element is a cause of the others. Nonetheless, for those who wish to use political science as a practical discipline for changing or preserving political arrangements, any leverage at any point of a system may be expected to assist corresponding adjustments elsewhere.

ENEMIES

Despite the advantages of democracy, there are deep and possibly irresolvable problems in democratic legitimation of the kind I have described. If legitimation and identification are inextricably related processes, or different dimensions of a single complex process, then democracy may provide the most accessible and effective way for maximising the possibilities of citizen self-identification. In a democracy, the mass of people are provided with the greatest opportunities to cultivate their identity as citizens. The same point may be made from the other side by saying that when citizenship is thus cultivated, the term democracy is a useful way of describing such a condition of things. But the very processes which maximise the likelihood of coherence between citizen legitimation and ruler legitimation, contain also possibilities of other dissonances within a polity.

K. Anthony Appiah has discussed the way in which recognition is sought not just from those with whom we identify, but from those from whom we distinguish ourselves.[45] This seems for Appiah to be so for two reasons: as both those with whom we identify and those from whom we distinguish ourselves are part of our social development, we cannot identify ourselves without reference to them; as we

---

[44] Ian McAllister, 'Keeping them Honest: Public and Elite Perceptions of Ethical Conduct among Australian Legislators', *Political Studies* 48, 1 (March 2000), 22–37, p. 35.

[45] In Charles Taylor, *Multiculturalism: Examining The Politics of Recognition*, ed. Amy Gutman, 2nd edn (Princeton, Princeton University Press, 1994).

see ourselves as to some extent disadvantaged in relation to them, their acknowledgement of our identity is part of a process of moving towards equality. The role of others which Appiah describes is supportive, potentially supportive, or at least 'dialogical'. Another role is not at all supportive, or rather it functions positively by being not supportive but antagonistic. We identify ourselves in this sense by comparing ourselves with others, by contrasting ourselves with others who are in some sense enemies. Since legitimation is so powerful a process, being part of the sustaining of government and hence of the mobilisation and use of coercion, the presence of antagonism and the depiction of hostile others as perhaps an unavoidable part of the legitimating identification process, suggests that one aspect of government will always be ground for misgiving.

The stronger the identification, the more exclusive, and the greater the tension and conflict between the dominant character, and all others. This is so because one way in which people may legitimate their own identities is by cultivating an enemy identity with which to contrast their own. The obverse of intense citizen identification is the symbolic creation of enemies, the gremlin in the machinery of democracy. This is the democratic paradox which is intensified if one community, or ethnic group, or party, or religion is uniquely associated with the legitimating identifications, or if it tries to be so. It may increase its own partisan advantage, but it weakens the overall unity of the state. This is a greater problem the greater the diversity of the governed community. In a multicultural society, identification and its obverse, the depiction of enemies, seem to anticipate conflict and/or oppression. The problem is one which had become more evident by the end of the twentieth century, both with a proliferating assertion of cultural, religious, and national identities, and with multinational or transnational forms of government such as the European Union.

The creation of identity also involves the creation of hostile or alien identities. The identity of a group is both sustained and threatened by the presentation of minorities of one kind and another as representing alternative, conflicting, disruptive or minatory identities. Thus the events surrounding the various attempts of New Age travellers in the United Kingdom to reach Stonehenge for the summer solstice in the years 1985–92 involved both the cultivation of a myth of the travellers as folk devils,[46] and an assertion of the identity of 'established' groups and cultures. The prime minister, Margaret Thatcher, proclaimed her intention to 'make life difficult for such things as hippy convoys',[47] whilst the home secretary, Douglas Hurd, described the travellers as 'A band of medieval brigands who have no respect for law and order and the rights of others.'[48]

The use of the law and of the officials and institutions of government to 'make life difficult' for eccentric groups was the obverse side of the proliferating assertions of national identity in Europe in the 1980s and 1990s. In the new Czech Republic, municipal authorities in North Bohemia called for new powers to enable them to force gypsies, whom they described as 'unwanted' elements, to move to Slovakia from where it was alleged they had come. 'We are talking about areas where civilisation is disintegrating', claimed Lukas Masin, mayor of Usti nad Labem. The prosecutor general of the Czech Republic, Jiri Setina, meanwhile asked the national parliament, at the beginning of January 1993, to approve measures enabling police to search private premises in application of a five-day limit on visits to them by persons other than relatives, and to oblige visitors to obtain approval from the local authorities. Borek Valvoda, mayor of Most, argued that these extra powers 'have nothing to do with gypsies as such, the point would be to reintroduce law and order'.[49] Order in such usage is a package with a substantial cultural content. Such conflict between legitimated identities can be as much a creation of government, or of citizenship, as a response or reaction of governors or citizens. It can lead to such antagonism that the groups depicted as hostile, even though their alien identification has been cultivated to serve the purposes of others, are ejected by those very people whose self-identification

---

[46] The phrase was originally used by Cohen to describe the depiction of Mods and Rockers, Stanley Cohen, *Folk Devils and Moral Panics: The Creation of the Mods and Rockers* (London, McGibbon and Kee, 1972).

[47] National Council for Civil Liberties, *Stonehenge. A Report into the Civil Liberties Implications of the Events Relating to the Convoys of Summer 1985 and 1986* (London, National Council for Civil Liberties, 1986), p. 1.

[48] June 1986, Quoted in ibid., p. 33.

[49] Adrian Bridge, 'Czech "Civilisation" Demands Gypsy Expulsions', *The Independent*, 13 January 1993, 10.

their presence sustains. If custodians regard a part of the human aggregate which they rule as not part of the governed community, they will subordinate or marginalise it, but they will not normally seek to dispense with it. If they do, they will attempt to keep the territory and dispense with the people.

If legitimation is inextricably involved with identification, how can there be legitimation or therefore stable government in a multi-cultural society? The problem arises from the place of enemies in the cultivation of identity. The solution of Richard Rorty, for liberal irony and solidarity in the public sphere, and contingent loyalties in the private will hardly work in the modern world where religious, ethnic, and cultural identifications are loud, insistent, and very public.[50] Liah Greenfeld and S. H. Beer, the one in a general sense, the other in specific praise of the American republic, have described a form of identification which perceives liberal tolerance not as a neutral value holding a multicultural society from above and outside, but as the most general culturally specific characteristic of that society.[51] To be American in this sense is not to be Protestant, or White, or Black, or Hispanic, but to recognise all of these identities whilst also claiming a historically contingent American identity which is not universal, which arises from a particular history and particular negotiations, victories, defeats, and compromises, but which entails one particular version of liberal tolerance in its mode of government and citizen activity.

The existence of diverse identification has no simple and predictable consequence for either orderly government or political peace. The confirmation of self-identification by contrast with others who are perceived as different is not necessarily synonymous with the symbolic cultivation of enemies. When diversity fragments potentially powerful and antagonistic identifications, it may work for stability. Where it intensifies the demands for internal control of other members or claimed members of the group, and the external hostility towards other groups who are perceived as different,

---

[50] Richard Rorty, *Contingency, Irony and Solidarity* (Cambridge, Cambridge University Press, 1989).
[51] Liah Greenfeld, *Nationalism: Five Roads to Modernity* (New Haven and London, Harvard University Press, 1992); Samuel H. Beer, *To Make A Nation: The Rediscovery of American Federalism* (London, Harvard University Press, 1993).

it may work for disruption and conflict. Though consociational democracy and other reformed democratic structures and forms of constitutional pluralism are both proposed as responses, it is not clear that such constitutional solutions can by themselves achieve peaceful politics.

TWO MODELS OF A COHERENTLY LEGITIMATING POLITY

Democracy takes two principal forms, or has two principal dimensions: rule by the people, and majority rule. And whilst the second contains the possibilities of the egregious cultivation of citizen identity and of enemies, the first contains the possibilities of citizen identification which is loosely textured, variegated, flexible, and dynamic. The cohesion of a polity with varieties of subject identification can be strengthened if the symbols of citizen identity are distinct from those of a partisan or sectarian character. If democracy is rule by the people, rather than rule by the majority, then the legitimating identities of rulers will need to be either restrained or complex. There can, in other words, be something to be said for the bland or the diverse. The choice is between a politics and a government of vision and a politics and a government of voices. Vision concentrates everything on a single image of the nation, the people, or the public destiny. Voices on the other hand accepts that variety and a certain incoherence is an inevitable feature of any real political community, and that government by the people, as opposed to rule by a dominant majority, involves some conciliation, negotiation, and mutual tolerance. Voices may go further, and articulate a social habitat which consists of more than one governed community, or of citizens governed at different levels or spheres in different ways, and with varied or multilayered citizen identifications. Such a multiple citizen identification could occur in federal states, or in states which were part of international or transnational government, such as the European Union. Vision and voices thus represent not only two different conceptions of legitimation, but two different conceptions of democracy. The distinction is, of course, set within a long tradition of similar categories: Michael Oakeshott's enterprises and associations, plural and monolithic polities, Arendt Lijphart's majoritarian and consociational or consensual democracies, Anthony D. Smith's civic, ethnic, and plural nations, Liah Greenfeld's two types of nationalism, ethnic and civic.[52]

Democratic legitimacy

Vision	Voices
Majority rule	Rule by the people
Partisan state style, head of state, rituals, etc.	Non-partisan head of state style, rituals etc.
Party = nation	Party is NOT the nation
Intense state	Bland state
Charisma	Convenience
High mobilisation	Low mobilisation
Enemies	Others

One of the main institutions for identification in a democracy is the political party. But parties may influence cohesion between ruler identification and citizen identification in very different ways. If rulers are so permanently entrenched that the fusion of their identification as rulers and that of their party appear to be a permanent feature of government, rather than a temporary consequence of electoral fortunes, then other groups and other parties may experience growing discord between their own identification and that of their rulers. If, by contrast, party identification is occasionally associated with rule, occasionally with opposition, coherence is less likely to be threatened. Rulers then have the role of voices in a varied governmental and political discourse, rather than visionaries with a single and exclusive identification.

An argument can be advanced in favour of vision and against voices. More identification means intenser but narrower legitimation. A state which is wholly neutral about the identifying concerns of its subjects may avoid alienating, but it is argued by some that it will not be viewed by them as in any particular sense their state,

---

[52] Michael Oakeshott, *On Human Conduct* (Oxford, Clarendon Press, 1975); Arend Lijphart, *Democracy in Plural Societies* (New Haven, Yale University Press, 1977); Anthony D. Smith, *National Identity* (London, Penguin, 1991); Greenfeld, *Nationalism*.

and will thus legitimate itself with difficulty. Green and Whiting comment on the absence of any particular cultural identity in the late twentieth-century British state: 'the British state is today quite self-consciously and increasingly less of a *good* state. That is, it has become less and less of a state which publicly sustains any explicit, coherent and integrated notion of the good in British society.'[53] This decline in the association of the state with a particular identity is then associated with declining compliance with law.[54] But it can be argued conversely that a ruling character that is either civic, or bland, or multifaceted is capable of existing profitably with a varied society in a way that a 'good' state is not. In that case, the history of the United Kingdom over the past 200 years is a history of a broad though punctuated move away from 'goodness' and towards multiplicity, and the secular and 'amoral' constitution of the United States is a valuable arrangement for preserving social order in a varied society.

CONCLUSION

Democratic legitimation, far from being a utopian or revolutionary ideal, is a practical and realistic means of minimising the problems of government and politics, and of creating a form of both which has many attractive features, both for subjects and for other states.

The claim I make for democracy is thus both modest and limited. I have not claimed any other virtues for democracy, though there are many which might be claimed. I have not tried to argue that democracy gives less corrupt, or more efficient, or more economically effective, or cheaper government, only that it seems the least ineffective way of achieving or sustaining congruence between popular self-identifications and the legitimating identities of rulers. Nor have I claimed that a government which enjoys legitimating identity congruence with as large a number as possible of its subjects is necessarily more stable than one which has such congruence with a smaller but more powerful section of the population. Legitimated democracies in this sense are not immune to military

[53] S. J. D. Green and R. C Whiting (eds.), *The Boundaries of the State in Modern Britain* (Cambridge, Cambridge University Press, 1996), p. 386.
[54] Ibid., p. 333.

coups, foreign subversion, or elite take-over. And I have of course made the wholly unargued prior assumption that a congruence of citizens' and rulers' legitimations is something worth having, and worth preserving. But since the evidence from all societies suggests that this assumption is one which people actually hold, the onus of proof is on those who would argue to the contrary.

The legitimation of rulers in their own eyes is of even greater importance to them than their legitimation in the eyes of their subjects. Democracy sustains government which is least likely to ignore the cultivated identifications, aspirations, and aversions of subjects not because of any contractual consent, but because it is a political system which makes difficult substantial and sustained disparities between the legitimated identity of rulers and that of subjects. The most immediately potent form of legitimation is the confirmation, in their own eyes, of the authoritative identity of rulers. But that identity is most likely to be challenged in democracies where dissonance between the legitimations of rulers and the legitimations of ordinary subjects and citizens is both most readily articulated and most readily redressed.

CHAPTER 7

Conclusion

The central place of self-legitimation in the activity of government has implications both for how we understand the activity of governing, and for what we can reasonably expect from it. Governing is not for those most directly involved in it only an instrumental activity but, like William Morris's useful work, inherently satisfying, an end in itself. As a self-sufficient activity in this sense, the activity of ruling or governing involves the cultivation of a distinctive identity which both depicts and justifies ruling. Endogenous self-legitimation acts as an identification which justifies and explains the actions of rulers, and each dimension, justification and explanation sustains the other. If the greatest investment in legitimation is endogenous rather than exogenous, arguments about legitimation as involving the recognition or acknowledgement or approval of the qualities or qualifications of rulers need recasting. It is not so much recognition in the market place or the street, or on the television or computer screen that will frequently be sought, as much as recognition in the embassy, the legislature, the council chamber or the presidential palace. This helps to explain the relative importance for rulers of relations, on the one hand, with other states and governing organisations and, on the other, with their subjects. It contributes to answering the question 'Why do rulers bother with endogenous self-legitimation?' 'Why are they not cynically manipulative, keeping legitimation solely for public use?' On one view of politics, that is of course exactly what they do do.[1] But in that case

---

[1] J. Rayner, 'Philosophy into Dogma: the Revival of Cultural Conservatism', *British Journal of Political Science* 16, 4 (October 1986), 455–74, argues that in order to succeed the leaders of belief have to encourage views which they do not themselves hold. Such a view, if not

everything outside the immediate public gaze would be utilitarian and informal, and it is not. Legitimation is important to rulers for the cultivation of their own identification, quite apart from any conventionally instrumental function it may have.

This does not mean that there is no instrumental dimension to government, nor that this dimension can be relegated to a lower level of significance. But the instrumental dimension does not comprise the whole of the activity of governing, nor always even its essential elements. Michael Rosen's question as to why subjects obey and how that obedience is justified can be complemented by a question as to why rulers bother to rule, and what are their own satisfactions and self-justifications. Just as the activity of ruling has an endogenous character, so it has an endogenous justification or legitimating self-description. Whether or not a politics of great causes lies in the past rather than the future – and there was more reason to believe this towards the end of the twentieth century than at its conclusion – we should not expect a government of mere housekeeping to be the pattern of the future. There is no evidence to suggests that there will not always be those who seek to govern and in so doing to legitimate their power and cultivate their distinctive governing identity. This aspect of governing may well induce a democratic, anarchic or liberal scepticism. Citizens need to be on their guard. Their agenda is not necessarily at all the same as that of their rulers.

There is an unavoidable logic in the self-legitimation of rulers and their cultivation of distinctive and, to that extent, alienating identities. The implications of this account are not encouraging for liberals, or at least not encouraging for the sort of expectations liberals have of *how* what they want can be brought about, and what its conditions and foundations will be. A politics of legitimation and identification will also be a politics of enemies and cultures which, however much they may be clothed in reason, are not founded upon it. If the analysis of this book is correct, then identity, and hence legitimation and government, will always rest on the cultivation of something which is distinctive, and which moreover

determined, is certainly made very likely, by a view which sees legitimation as a claim made only by rulers to subjects.

will be sustained to a greater or lesser degree by the depiction of enemies.

It could be asked how the account given in this book could be tested. What for instance could be shown by a time log of randomly chosen governors or clusters of governors? There are several difficulties with such a programme. Access would be difficult or impossible. It would require permanent shadowing. Nor could an audit of time or expenditure do the job, since legitimation is not a distinct and autonomous activity, but a dimension of most or all government. In that sense whilst some such testing might be illuminating, it could not 'prove' what is an alternative narrative, rather than a testable empirical hypothesis. It might even, paradoxically, be the case that democratic regimes would be less open to this kind of examination. The private ostentations of monarchs were not necessarily hidden, even though they were part of their private self-creation rather than of their public display. The private ostentations of presidents and prime ministers may specifically be concealed from public view, both because they might be criticised or ridiculed, and because it is part of their character and justification that they are *not* accessible to ordinary people. This creates difficulties for pursuing what is a largely unpursued suggestion of the preceding argument: that there is a significant relation between the manner of endogenous legitimation and other features of government. The account of legitimating identities is best seen not as a theory of government which could be tested, but rather as an account of government which can be used to provide a different and to that extent fuller understanding of what governments and rulers are doing.

The conclusion to be drawn from the argument of this book is not that legitimation is an irrational process. The pursuit of theories to explain what kinds of legitimation work, and what do not, does not have to succumb before emotion or arbitrariness. But the kinds of questions which are most worthwhile asking will not take as their premise a concept of a utility maximising individual, though a well-being and coherent identity maximising individual would provide a sound premise. This is not because an emphasis on individuals is unhelpful but because, in the matter of legitimation it is more illuminating to pay attention to those aspects of politics which involve identity seeking. Unless this is done, a large slice of political conduct will seem either incomprehensible or irrelevant, which offends democratic empiricism since to the people themselves it is neither.

This book has not addressed the question, which has enjoyed the attention of many of those who have written on authority and the legitimation of government, of the relation of legitimation to obedience, or resistance, to the commands of rulers. But two contributions to such a discussion nonetheless arise from the features of legitimation which have been considered here. First, legitimation is an aspect of the action of obeying, or not obeying. Second, a coherent sense of identity appears to be generally sought by political actors, to be a good or a utility which they either seek, or strive to preserve and cultivate. An observation of this fact helps an understanding not just of the behaviour of subjects towards domestic government, but of the behaviour of states towards each other.

Rulers and leaders who legitimate themselves endogenously with little or no regard for the forms of legitimation which will be comprehensible to, and will accord with the identifications of, those whom they rule are cultivating a difficulty for their own government. Such an understanding of the relation between endogenous legitimation and the identification of subjects will not necessarily make possible prediction of tensions and breakdowns, but it will assist the understanding of those that occur.

There is every reason to try to construct an account of legitimation which will assist the understanding of government success and failure, and which will increase our understanding of why some things work and others do not. So the self-absorption of rulers, though endemic to and a characterising feature of government, has at least the self-defeating feature that the more purely self-referential it is, the less is it able to ensure the conditions necessary for its own continuation. Democracy may not work in quite the way its normative advocates propose or expect. But it is the best way available of checking the inconvenient consequences of the self-legitimation of rulers. It works to beneficial ends which may not be the ends of any of the parties to the process, but which are nonetheless to the general good.

If predictions of less state *dirigisme* after the year 2000 are accurate, that will not necessarily mean less government. Social scientists should keep a sharp look out for the trappings of office, which are the symptoms of government. 'By their fruits ye shall know them.' But not only by their fruits, but also by their suits, by their pomp and their circumstance. It was pointed out many years ago when Desmond Morris described humans as naked apes[2] that humans were in fact not naked, but clothed, and that the construction of artefacts for use and display was a characteristic of the species. Virginia Woolf made a similar point when discussing the elaborate feathered finery of the male establishment in *Three Guineas*.[3] An academic study of the politics of clothing may be some way off, but as an indication of the estimate made by rulers of their own importance, and thus of the extent of the time and resources devoted to maintaining that sense of importance, observation of the external trappings of governing will prove to be, at the very least, evidence of the continuing vigour of the activity of governing into the new century. When Paine dismissed Burke for pitying the feathers but forgetting the dying bird, he made a sharp polemical point. But he diverted attention from the fact that without the feathers, the bird is scarcely a bird at all, and that if we want to go birdwatching, or regime spotting, one of the most reliable indicators to keep our eyes peeled for is the plumage.

[2] Desmond Morris, *The Naked Ape* (London, Jonathan Cape, 1967).
[3] Virginia Woolf, *Three Guineas* (London, Hogarth Press, 1938, repr. London, Penguin, 1993).

Bibliography

Abercrombie, Nicholas and Turner, Bryan S., 'The Dominant Ideology Thesis' in Anthony Giddens and David Held (eds.), *Classes, Power, and Conflict: Classical and Contemporary Debates*, Berkeley: University of California Press, 1982.

Abercrombie, Nicholas, Hill, Stephen, and Turner, Bryan S. (eds.), *Dominant Ideologies*, London: Unwin Hyman, 1990.

Abromeit, Heidrun, *Democracy in Europe: Legitimising Politics in a Non-State Polity*, Oxford: Berghahn Books, 1998.

Agulhon, Maurice, 'Politics, Images, and Symbols in Post-Revolutionary France' in Sean Wilentz (ed.), *Rites of Power: Symbolism, Ritual and Politics Since the Middle Ages*, Philadelphia: University of Pennsylvania Press, 1985.

Ahmad, Aijaz, *In Theory: Classes, Nations, Literatures*, London: Verso, 1992.

Aho, James A., *This Thing of Darkness: A Sociology of the Enemy*, Seattle: University of Washington Press, 1994.

The Politics of Righteousness: Idaho Christian Patriotism, Seattle: University of Washington Press, 1995.

Alagappa, Muthiah, *Democratic Transition in Asia: The Role of the International Community*, Honolulu, Hawaii: East-West Center, 1994.

Political Legitimacy in Southeast Asia: The Quest for Moral Authority, Stanford: Stanford University Press, 1995.

Albertoni, E. A., *Mosca and the Theory of Elitism*, Oxford: Blackwell, 1987.

Anderson, Benedict R. O'G., 'The Idea of Power in Javanese Culture' in Claire Holt (ed.), with the assistance of Benedict R. O'G. Anderson and James Siegel, *Culture and Politics in Indonesia*, Ithaca: Cornell University Press, 1972.

Anglade, Christian, *Sources of Legitimacy in Latin America: The Mechanisms of Consensus in Exclusionary Societies* (Essex Papers in Politics & Government no. 38), Essex: University of Essex, 1987.

Anglo, Sydney, 'The Hampton Court Painting of the Field of the Cloth of Gold', *The Antiquaries Journal* 46 (1966), 287–307.

Images of Tudor Kingship, London: B. A. Seaby, 1992.

Appiah, K. Anthony, 'Identity, Authenticity, Survival: Multicultural Societies and Social Reproduction' in Charles Taylor, *Multiculturalism: Examining the Politics of Recognition* (ed.) Amy Gutmann, Princeton: Princeton University Press, 1994.

Arblaster, Anthony, 'Taking Monarchy Seriously', *New Left Review* 174 (1989), 97–110.

Ascherson, Neal, 'The Spectre of Popular Sovereignty Looms over Greater England', *The Independent on Sunday*, 18 November 1990.

Austin, Regina, 'The Problem of Legitimacy in the Welfare State', *University of Pennsylvania Law Review* 130 (1982), 1510–18.

Bairner, Alan, 'The Battlefield of Ideas: The Legitimation of Political Violence in Northern Ireland', *European Journal of Political Research* 14 (1986), 633–49.

Baldwin, Robert, *Rules and Government*, Oxford: Oxford University Press, 1995.

Barker, Rodney, 'Harold Laski' in Walter Euchner (ed.), *Klassiker des Sozialismus II*, Munich: C. H. Beck, 1989.

Political Legitimacy and the State, Oxford: Clarendon Press, 1990.

'Citizenship, Legitimacy and Cultural Pluralism in Britain' in Richard Nile (ed.), *Immigration and the Politics of Ethnicity and Race in Australia and Britain*, London: Centre for Australian Studies, 1991.

'Civil Disobedience as Persuasion: Dworkin and Greenham Common', *Political Studies* 40, 2 (June 1992), 290–8.

'Legitimacy in the United Kingdom: Scotland and the Poll Tax', *British Journal of Political Science* 22, 4 (October 1992), 521–33.

'Legitimacy: The Identity of the Accused', *Political Studies* 42, 1 (1994), 101–2.

'Four Dimensions of Political Identity: A Theory of Legitimacy' in Patrick Dunleavy and Jeffrey Stanyer (eds.), *Contemporary Political Studies 1994*, Belfast: Political Studies Association, 1994.

'National and Ethnic Minorities in the United Kingdom and the Legitimacy of the State' in Jagdish Gundara and Michael Twaddel (eds.), *Multiculturalism and the State*, London: Institute of Commonwealth Studies, 1994.

'Whose Legitimacy? Elites, Nationalism and Ethnicity in the United Kingdom', *New Community* 21, 2 (April 1995), 207–14.

'Pluralism, Revenant or Recessive?' in Jack Hayward, Brian Barry, and Archie Brown (eds.), *The British Study of Politics in the Twentieth Century*, Oxford: Oxford University Press, 1999.

'Hooks and Hands, Interests and Enemies: Political Thinking as Political Action', *Political Studies* 48, 2, Special Issue (2000), 223–38.

'The Long Millennium, the Short Century, and the Persistence of Legitimation', *Contemporary Politics* 6, 1 (2000), 7–12.

Barnett, Michael N., 'Bringing in the New World Order: Liberalism, Legitimacy, and the United Nations', *World Politics* 49, 4 (July 1997), 526–51.

Barry, Brian, *Sociologists, Economists, and Democracy*, London: Collier-Macmillan, 1970.

Bastid, P., 'L'Idée de légitimité' in P. Bastid *et al.*, *L'Idée de légitimité*, Paris: Presses Universitaires de France, 1967.

Baylis, Thomas S., *The Technical Intelligentsia and the East German Elite: Legitimacy and Social Change under Mature Communism*, Berkeley: University of California Press, 1974.

Bealey, F., 'Stability and Crisis: Fears about Threats to Democracy', *European Journal of Political Research* 15 (1987), 687–715.

Beetham, David, *Max Weber and the Theory of Modern Politics*, London: George Allen and Unwin, 1974.

    The Legitimation of Power, London: Macmillan, 1991.

    'In Defence of Legitimacy', *Political Studies* 41, 3 (September 1993), 488–91.

Beetham, David and Lord, Christopher, *Legitimacy and the European Union*, London: Longman, 1998.

Bendix, R. and Roth, G. (eds.), *Scholarship & Partisanship: Essays on Max Weber*, Berkeley: University of California Press, 1971.

Benhabib, Seyla, 'Towards a Deliberative Model of Democratic Legitimacy' in Seyla Benhabib (ed.), *Democracy and Difference: Contesting the Boundaries of the Political*, Princeton: Princeton University Press, 1996.

Bensman, Joseph, 'Max Weber's Concept of Legitimacy: An Evaluation' in Arthur J. Vidich and Ronald Glassman (eds.), *Conflict and Control: Challenges to Legitimacy of Modern Governments*, Beverley Hills: Sage, 1979.

Bensman, Joseph and Givant, Michael, 'Charisma and Modernity: The Use and Abuse of a Concept' in Ronald M. Glassman and William H. Swatos (eds.), *Charisma, History, and Social Structure*, New York: Greenwood Press, 1986.

Berger, Joseph and Zelditch, Morris, *Status, Power and Legitimacy*, London: Transaction Books, 1996.

Berger, Peter L., *The Sacred Canopy: Elements of a Sociological Theory of Religion*, Garden City, NY: Doubleday, 1967.

Binski, Paul, *Westminster Abbey and the Plantagenets*, New Haven: Yale University Press, 1995.

Birch. A. H., 'Overload, Ungovernability and Delegitimation: The Theories and the British Case', *British Journal of Political Science* 14, 2 (1984), 135–60.

Birkinshaw, Patrick, Harden, Ian, and Lewis, Norman, *Government By Moonlight: The Hybrid Parts of the State*, London: Unwin Hyman, 1990.

Birnbaum, Norman, 'Monarchies and Sociologists: A Reply to Professor Shils and Mr. Young', *Sociological Review*, new series 3 (1955), 5–23.

Black, Antony, 'Classical Islam and Medieval Europe: A Comparison of Political Philosophies and Cultures', *Political Studies* 41, 1 (March 1993), 58–69.

Black, David and Klotz, Audie, *International Legitimation and Domestic Political Change: Implications for South African Foreign Relations*, Bellville: University of Western Cape, 1995.

Blau, Peter M., 'Critical Remarks on Weber's Theory of Authority', *American Political Science Review* 57, 2 (June 1963), 305–16.

Blondel, Jean, Sinnott, Richard and Svensson, Palle, *People and Parliament in the European Union: Participation, Democracy, and Legitimacy*, Oxford: Clarendon Press, 1998.

Bourdieu, Pierre, *Language and Symbolic Power*, ed. John B. Thompson, trans. Gino Raymond and Matthew Adamson, Cambridge: Polity Press, 1991.

  The State Nobility: Elite Schools in the Field of Power, trans. Lauretta Clough, Cambridge: Polity Press, 1996.

Bourricaud, François, 'Legitimacy and Legitimation', *Current Sociology* 35, 2 (1987), 57–67.

Brazier, Margaret, Lovecy, Jill, Moran, Michael, and Potton, Margaret, 'Falling from a Tightrope: Doctors and Lawyers Between the Market and the State', *Political Studies* 41, 2 (June 1993), 197–213.

Bridge, Adrian, 'Czech "Civilisation" Demands Gypsy Expulsions', *The Independent*, 13 January 1993.

Brown, David, *The Legitimacy of Governments in Plural Societies* (Occasional Paper No. 43), Singapore: Department of Political Science, National University of Singapore, 1984.

Bryan, Dominic, *Orange Parades: The Politics of Ritual, Tradition and Control*, London: Pluto, 2000.

Búrca, Grainne de, 'The Quest for Legitimacy in the European Union', *Modern Law Review* 59 (1996), 349–76.

Burke, Peter, *The Fabrication of Louis XIV*, New Haven: Yale University Press, 1992.

Callaway, Helen, 'Purity and Exotica in Legitimating the Empire. Cultural Constructions of Gender, Sexuality and Race' in Terence Ranger and Olufemi Vaughan (eds.), *Legitimacy and the State in Twentieth-Century Africa: Essays in Honour of A. H. M. Kirk-Greene*, London: Macmillan, 1993.

Campbell, David, 'Truth Claims and Value-Freedom in the Treatment of Legitimacy: The Case of Weber', *Journal of Law and Society* 13, 2 (Summer 1986), 207–24.

Cannadine, David, 'The Context, Performance and Meaning of Ritual: the British Monarchy and the "Invention of Tradition", c. 1820–1977' in Eric Hobsbawm and Terence Ranger (eds.), *The Invention of Tradition*, Cambridge: Cambridge University Press, 1983.

Cannadine, David and Price, Simon (eds.), *Rituals of Royalty: Power and Ceremonial in Traditional Societies*, Cambridge: Cambridge University Press, 1987.

Carrington, Charles, *Rudyard Kipling: His Life and Work*, London: Macmillan, 1955, Harmondsworth: Penguin, 1970.

Chan, Hok-lam, *Legitimation in Imperial China: Discussions under the Jurchen-Chin Dynasty [1115–1234]*, London: University of Washington Press, 1984.

Choueiri, Y. M., 'Theoretical Paradigms of Islamic Movements', *Political Studies* 41, 4 (March 1993), 108–16.

Chryssochoou, Dimitris N., *Democracy in the European Union*, London: Tauris Academic Studies, 1998.

Cipriani, Roberto, 'The Sociology of Legitimation: An Introduction', *Current Sociology* 35, 2 (1987), 1–20.

Claude, Inis L., Jr, 'Collective Legitimization as a Political Function of the United Nations', *International Organization* 20 (1966), 367–79.

Cohen, J., 'Deliberation and Democratic Legitimacy' in Alan P. Hamlin and Philip Pettit, *The Good Polity: Normative Analysis of the State*, Oxford: Blackwell, 1989.

Cohen, Ronald and Toland, Judith D. (eds.), *State Formation and Political Legitimacy*. Political Anthropology 6, New Brunswick: Transaction Books, 1988.

Cohen, Stanley, *Folk Devils and Moral Panics: the Creation of the Mods and Rockers*, London: McGibbon & Kee, 1972.

Connolly, William (ed.), *Legitimacy and the State*, Oxford: Blackwell, 1984.

Connor, Walker, 'Nationalism and Political Legitimacy', *Canadian Review of Studies in Nationalism* 8, 2 (1981), 201–28.

deJasay, Anthony, *The State*, Oxford: Blackwell, 1985.

Deringil, Selim, *The Well-Protected Domains: Ideology and the Legitimation of Power in the Ottoman Empire, 1876–1909*, London: I. B. Tauris, 1998.

Deutsch, Karl, 'The Commitment of National Legitimacy Symbols as a Verification Technique', *The Journal of Conflict Resolution* 7, 3 (September 1963), 360–9.

Di Palma, Guiseppe, 'Legitimation from the Top to Civil Society: Politico-Cultural Change in Eastern Europe', *World Politics* 44, 1 (October 1991), 49–80.

Downs, Anthony, *An Economic Theory of Democracy*, New York: Harper and Brothers, 1957.

146 *Bibliography*

Drake, Helen, 'The European Commission and the Politics of Legitimacy in the European Union' in Neill Nugent (ed.), *At the Heart of the Union: Studies of the European Commission*, London: Macmillan, 1997.

Dryzek, John S., *Discursive Democracy: Politics, Policy and Political Science*, New York: Cambridge University Press, 1990.

Dunleavy, Patrick, 'Quasi-governmental Professionalism: Some Implications for Public Policy-making in Britain' in Anthony Barker (ed.), *Quangos in Britain: Government and the Networks of Public Policy Making*, London: Macmillan, 1982.

  Democracy, Bureaucracy and Public Choice: Economic Explanations in Political Science, Hemel Hempstead: Harvester Wheatsheaf, 1991.

Dyzenhaus, David, *Legality and Legitimacy: Carl Schmitt, Hans Kelsen and Herman Heller in Weimar*, Oxford: Clarendon Press, 1997.

Easton, David, *A Systems Analysis of Political Life*, New York: John Wiley and Sons, 1965.

Eckstein, H., *Support for Regimes: Theories and Tests*. Centre for International Studies, Woodrow Wilson School of Public and International Affairs, Research Monograph 44, Princeton: Center for International Studies, 1979.

Edelman, Murray, *The Symbolic Uses of Politics*, London: University of Illinois Press, 1964.

  'Space and the Social Order', *Journal of Architectural Education* 32, 3 (November 1978), 2–7.

Elias, Norbert, *The Court Society*, trans. Edmund Jephcott, 1st edn 1969, Oxford: Blackwell, 1983.

Fagin, Adam, 'Democratization in Eastern Europe: The Limitations of the Existing Transition Literature', *Contemporary Politics* 4, 2 (June 1998), 143–59.

Fatton, R. Jr, 'Gramsci and the Legitimization of the State: the Case of the Senegalese Passive Revolution', *Canadian Journal of Political Science* 19, 4 (1986), 729–50.

Ferrell, Lori Anne, *Government by Polemic: James I, the King's Preachers, and the Rhetorics of Conformity, 1603–1625*, Stanford: Stanford University Press, 1998.

Figgis, J. N., 'The Church and the Secular Theory of the State' (1905) in David Nicholls, *The Pluralist State: the Political Ideas of J. N. Figgis and His Contemporaries*, 2nd edn, London: Macmillan, 1994.

Franck, Thomas M., *The Power of Legitimacy Among Nations*, New York: Oxford University Press, 1990.

Friedrich, Carl J., 'Political Leadership and the Problem of Charismatic Power', *The Journal of Politics* 23 (1961), 3–24.

  Man and His Government, New York: McGraw Hill, 1963.

Fukuyama, Francis, *The End of History and the Last Man*, London: Hamish Hamilton, 1992.

Fulbrook, Mary, *The Divided Nation: A History of Germany, 1918–1990*, Oxford: Oxford University Press, 1992.

Garcia, Soledad (ed.), *European Identity and the Search for Legitimacy*, London: Pinter, 1993.

Geertz, Clifford, *Negara: The Theatre State in Nineteenth Century Bali*, Princeton: Princeton University Press, 1980.

'Centres, Kings, and Charisma: Reflections on the Symbolics of Power' in Sean Wilentz (ed.), *Rites of Power: Symbolism, Ritual and Politics Since the Middle Ages*, Philadelphia: University of Pennsylvania Press, 1985.

Gerth, H. C. and Mills, C. W. (eds.), *From Max Weber: Essays in Sociology*, London: Routledge and Kegan Paul, 1948.

Gibson, James L. and Caldeira, Gregory A., 'Changes in the Legitimacy of the European Court of Justice: A Post-Maastricht Analysis', *British Journal of Political Science* 28, 1 (January 1998), 63–91.

Giddens, Anthony, '"Power" in the Recent Writings of Talcott Parsons', *Sociology* 2, 3 (1968), 257–72.

Studies in Social and Political Theory, London: Hutchinson, 1979.

A Contemporary Critique of Historical Materialism, London: Macmillan, 1981.

Gilbert, F. (ed.), *The Historical Essays of Otto Hintze*, New York: Oxford University Press, 1975.

Gilbert, Michelle, 'The Person of the King: Ritual and Power in a Ghanaian State' in David Cannadine and Simon Price (eds.), *Rituals of Royalty: Power and Ceremonial in Traditional Societies*, Cambridge: Cambridge University Press, 1987.

Glassman, Ronald L., 'Rational and Irrational Legitimacy' in Arthur J. Vidich and Ronald M. Glassman (eds.), *Conflict and Control: Challenges to Legitimacy of Modern Governments*, London: Sage, 1979.

Glassman, Ronald M. and Swatos, William H. (eds.), *Charisma, History, and Social Structure*, New York: Greenwood Press, 1986.

Goffman, E., *The Presentation of Self in Everyday Life*, New York: Doubleday, 1959.

Goodin, Robert E., 'Rites of Rulers' in Robert E. Goodin, *Manipulatory Politics*, New Haven and London: Yale University Press, 1980.

Goodsell, Charles, *The Social Meaning of Civic Space: Studying Political Authority through Architecture*, Lawrence: University Press of Kansas, 1988.

Gordon, Gillian, Monnas, Lisa, and Elam, Caroline (eds.), *The Regal Image of Richard II and the Wilton Diptych*, London: Harvey Miller Publishers, 1998.

Gorman, John, *Banner Bright*, Harmondsworth: Allen Lane, 1973.

Gow, James, *Legitimacy and the Military: The Yugoslav Crisis*, London: Pinter, 1993.

Gowan, P., 'The Origins of the Administrative Elite', *New Left Review* 162, March–April 1987, 4–34.

Grafstein, R., 'The Failure of Weber's Conception of Legitimacy', *Journal of Politics*, 43 (1981), 456–72.

Gramsci, Antonio, *Selections from the Prison Notebooks of Antonio Gramsci*, ed. and trans. Quintin Hoare and Geoffrey Nowell Smith, London: Lawrence and Wishart, 1971.

Green, Donald P. and Shapiro, Ian, *Pathologies of Rational Choice Theory: A Critique of Applications in Rational Choice Theory*, New Haven: Yale University Press, 1994.

Green, Leslie, *The Authority of the State*, Oxford: Clarendon Press, 1988.

Green, S. J. D. and Whiting, R. C. (eds.), *The Boundaries of the State in Modern Britain*, Cambridge: Cambridge University Press, 1996.

Graeger, Nina, *European Integration and the Legitimation of Supranational Power: Dilemas, Strategies and New Challenges*, Oslo: Department of Political Science, 1994.

Greenfeld, Liah, *Nationalism: Five Roads to Modernity*, New Haven and London: Harvard University Press, 1992.

Gurr, T. R., *Why Men Rebel*, Princeton: Princeton University Press, 1970.

Gyford, John, *Citizens, Consumers, and Councils: Local Government and the Public*, London: Macmillan, 1991.

Habermas, Jürgen, 'What Does A Crisis Mean Today? Legitimation Problems in Late Capitalism', *Social Research* 40 (1973), 643–67.

    Legitimation Crisis, trans. Thomas McCarthy, London: Heinemann, 1976.

    Between Facts and Norms: Contributions to a Discourse Theory of Law and Democracy, trans. William Rehg, Oxford: Polity Press, 1996.

Haddock, Bruce and Caraiani, Ovidiu, 'Nationalism and Civil Society in Romania', *Political Studies* 47, 2 (June 1999), 258–74.

Halliday, Fred, 'The Politics of Islam: A Second Look', *British Journal of Political Science* 25, 3 (July 1995), 399–417.

Halliwell, David, *Little Malcolm and his Struggle Against the Eunuchs*, London: Faber, 1967.

Hammerton, Elizabeth and Cannadine, David, 'Conflict and Consensus on a Ceremonial Occasion: The Diamond Jubilee in Cambridge in 1897', *Historical Journal* 24, 1 (1981), 111–46.

Hardin, Russell, *One for All: The Logic of Group Conflict*, Princeton: Princeton University Press, 1995.

Harington, Sir John, *Epigrams*, book 4, number 5, 1618.

Harlow, C., 'Power from the People? Representation and Constitutional Theory' in Patrick McAuslan and John McEldowney (eds.), *Law, Legitimacy and the Constitution*, London: Sweet and Maxwell, 1985.

Heisler, M. O. and Kvavik, Robert B., 'Patterns of European Politics: The "European Polity" Model' in M. O. Heisler (ed.), *Politics in Europe: Structures and Processes in Some Postindustrial Democracies*, New York: David McKay, 1974.

Held, David, 'Crisis Tendencies, Legitimation and the State' in John B. Thompson and David Held (eds.), *Habermas: Critical Debates*, London: Macmillan, 1982.

'Power and Legitimacy in Contemporary Britain' in Gregor McLennan, David Held and Stuart Hall (eds.), *State and Society in Contemporary Britain: a Critical Introduction*, Cambridge: Polity Press, 1984.

Models of Democracy, Cambridge: Polity Press, 1987.

Held, David, *et al.* (ed.), *States and Societies*, Oxford: Martin Robertson, 1983.

Henshaw, David, *Animal Warfare: The Story of the Animal Liberation Front*, London: Fontana/Collins, 1989.

Hilton, Tim, 'Between Heaven and Earth', *The Independent on Sunday: The Sunday Review*, September 1993, 28–9.

Hix, Simon, 'The Study of the European Union II: The "New Governance" Agenda and its Rival', *Journal of European Public Policy* 5, 1 (1998), 38–65.

Hobsbawm, Eric, *Primitive Rebels,* 3rd edn, Manchester: Manchester University Press, 1971.

Nations and Nationalism since 1780: Programme, Myth, Reality, Cambridge: Cambridge University Press, 1990.

Age of Extremes: The Short Twentieth Century 1914–1991, London: Michael Joseph, 1994.

Hobsbawm, Eric and Ranger, Terence, *The Invention of Tradition*, Cambridge: Cambridge University Press, 1983.

Holmes, Leslie, *The End of Communist Power: Anti-Corruption Campaigns and Legitimation Crisis*, Cambridge: Polity Press, 1993.

Post-Communism: An Introduction, Cambridge: Polity Press, 1997.

Hooghe, Liesbet, 'Images of Europe: Orientations to European Integration Among Senior Officials of the Commission', *British Journal of Political Science* 29, 2 (April 1999), 345–67.

Hroch, Miroslav, *Social Preconditions of National Revival in Europe: A Comparative Analysis of the Social Composition of Patriotic Groups among the Smaller European Nations*, trans. Ben Fowkes, Cambridge: Cambridge University Press, 1985.

'From National Movement to the Fully-formed Nation: the Nation-Building Process in Europe', *New Left Review* 198, March/April (1993), 3–20.

Huskey, Eugene, 'Comment on "The Logic of Collective Action in Soviet-type Societies"', *Journal of Soviet Nationalities* 1 (Summer 1990), 28.

Jachtenfuchs, Markus, 'Theoretical Perspectives on European Governance', *European Law Journal* 1, 2 (July 1995), 115–33.

Jacobs, Harold (ed.), *Weatherman*, New York: Ramparts Press, 1970.

James, Alan, *Sovereign Statehood: The Basis of International Society*, London: Allen and Unwin, 1986.

Jobert, Bruno and Muller, Pierre, *L'État en action: politiques publiques et corporatismes*, Paris: Presses Universitaires de France, 1987.

Johnson, T., 'The State and the Professions: Peculiarities of the British' in Anthony Giddens and G. Mackenzie (eds.), *Social Class and the Division of Labour: Essays in Honour of Ilya Neustadt*, Cambridge: Cambridge University Press, 1982.

Joll, James, *Gramsci*, London: Fontana/Collins, 1977.

Kaas, Max, Newton, Kenneth, and Scarbrough, Elinor, 'Beliefs in Government', *Politics* 17, 2 (May 1997), 135–39.

Kantorowicz, Ernst H., *The King's Two Bodies*, Princeton: Princeton University Press, 1957.

Käufeler, Heinz, *Modernization, Legitimacy and Social Movement: A Study of Socio-Cultural Dynamics and Revolution in Iran and Ethiopia*, Zurich: Ethnologische Schriften Zürich, 1988.

Kedward, H. R., *In Search of the Maquis: Rural Resistance in Southern France, 1942–1944*, Oxford: Oxford University Press, 1993.

Kepel, Gilles, *The Revenge of God: The Resurgence of Islam, Christianity and Judaism in the Modern World*, Cambridge: Polity Press, 1994.
  Allah in the West, Cambridge: Polity Press, 1997.

Kertzer, David L., *Ritual, Politics, and Power*, New Haven & London: Yale University Press, 1988.

Kipling, Gordon, *Enter the King: Theatre, Liturgy and Ritual in the Medieval Civic Triumph*, Oxford: Oxford University Press, 1986.

Kolankiewicz, George, 'The Other Europe: Different Roads to Modernity in Eastern and Central Europe' in Soledad Garcia (ed.), *European Identity and the Search for Legitimacy*, London: Pinter, 1993.

Kopstein, Jeffrey, 'Chipping Away at the State: Workers' Resistance and the Demise of East Germany', *World Politics* 48, 3 (1996), 391–423.

Kovats, Martin, 'The Political Significance of the First National Gypsy Minority Self-government in Hungary', *Contemporary Politics* 6, 3 (September 2000), 247–62.

Kubik, Jan, *The Power of Symbols against the Symbols of Power: The Rise of Solidarity and the Fall of State Socialism in Poland*, Pennsylvania: Pennsylvania State University Press, 1994.

Kymlicka, Will, *Multicultural Citizenship: A Liberal Theory of Minority Rights*, Oxford: Oxford University Press, 1995.

Kymlicka, Will (ed.), *The Rights of Minority Cultures*, Oxford: Oxford University Press, 1995.

Laffan, Brigid, 'The Politics of Identity and Political Order in Europe', *Journal of Common Market Studies* 34, 1 (March 1996), 81–103.

Lane, Christel, 'Legitimacy and Power in the Soviet Union through Socialist Ritual', *British Journal of Political Science* 14 (1984), 207–17.

The Rites of Rulers: Ritual in Industrial Society – the Soviet Case, Cambridge: Cambridge University Press, 1981.

Lane, Robert E., 'Experiencing Money and Experiencing Power' in Ian Shapiro and Grant Reeher (eds.), *Power, Inequality, and Democratic Politics: Essays in Honour of Robert A. Dahl*, Boulder and London: Westview Press, 1988.

Laski, H. J., *Studies in the Problem of Sovereignty*, London: George Allen & Unwin (repr. 1968) 1917.

The Foundations of Sovereignty and other Essays, London: Allen & Unwin 1922.

A Grammar of Politics, London: George Allen & Unwin, 1925.

Lasswell, Harold D. and Fox, Merritt B., *The Signature of Power: Buildings, Communication, and Policy*, New Brunswick, NJ: Transaction Books, 1979.

Lawrence, Jon, *Speaking for the People: Party, Language and Popular Politics in England 1867–1914*, Cambridge: Cambridge University Press, 1998.

Leeson, R. A., *Strike: A Live History 1887–1971*, London: George Allen & Unwin, 1973.

Lehning, Percy and Weale, Allbert (eds.), *Citizenship, Democracy and Justice in the New Europe*, London: Routledge, 1997.

Levi, Margaret, *Of Rule and Revenue*, London: University of California Press, 1988.

Lewis, Paul G., 'Obstacles to the Establishment of Political Legitimacy in Communist Poland', *British Journal of Political Science* 12 (April 1982), 125–47.

'Legitimation and Political Crises: East European Developments in the Post-Stalin Period' in Paul G. Lewis (ed.), *Eastern Europe: Political Crisis and Legitimation*, London: Croom Helm, 1984.

Lijphart, Arend, *Democracy in Plural Societies*, New Haven: Yale University Press, 1977.

Linz, Juan J., *The Breakdown of Democratic Regimes: Crisis, Breakdown, and Reequilibration*, Baltimore: Johns Hopkins University Press, 1978.

'Legitimacy of Democracy and the Socioeconomic System' in Mattei Dogan (ed.), *Comparing Pluralist Democracies: Strains on Legitimacy*, Boulder: Westview Press, 1988.

Lodge, Juliet, 'Transparency and Democratic Legitimacy', *Journal of Common Market Studies* 32 (1994), 343–68.

Luckmann, Thomas, 'Comments on Legitimation', *Current Sociology* 35, 2 (1987), 109–17.

Machiavelli, Niccolò, *The Prince*, 1532, Cambridge: Cambridge University Press, 1988.

Mackenzie, W. J. M., *Political Identity*, Harmondsworth: Penguin, 1978.

Markus, Maria, 'Overt and Covert Modes of Legitimation in East European Societies' in T. H. Rigby and Ference Feher (eds.), *Political Legitimation in Communist States*, London: Macmillan, 1982.

Marr, Andrew, 'IRA Must Stop This Idiocy', *The Observer*, 6 February 2000, 26.

Marshall, Geoffrey, *Constitutional Theory*, Oxford: Oxford University Press, 1971.

Matheson, C., 'Weber and the Classification of Forms of Legitimacy', *British Journal of Sociology* 2 (1987), 199–215.

McAllister, Ian, 'Keeping them Honest: Public and Elite Perceptions of Ethical Conduct among Australian Legislators', *Political Studies* 48, 1 (March 2000), 22–37.

McAuslan, Patrick, McEldowney, John F. (eds.), *Law, Legitimacy and the Constitution*, London: Sweet and Maxwell, 1985.

McCauley, Martin (ed.), 'Legitimation in the German Democratic Republic' in Paul G. Lewis (ed.), *Eastern Europe: Political Crisis and Legitimation*, London: Croom Helm, 1984.

McClelland, David C., *Power: the Inner Experience*, New York: Irvington Publishers, 1975.

McMullen, David, 'Bureaucrats and Cosmology: The Ritual Code of T'ang China' in David Cannadine and Simon Price (eds.), *Rituals of Royalty: Power and Ceremonial in Traditional Societies*, Cambridge: Cambridge University Press, 1987.

Merriam, Charles E., *Political Power: Its Composition and Incidence*, New York: Whittlesey House, McGraw-Hill, 1934.

Milne, A. A., *Now We are Six*, London: Methuen, 1927, 1989.

Mitchell, R. Judson, 'Leadership, Legitimacy, and Institutions in Post-Soviet Russia', *Mediterranean Quarterly* 4, 2 (Spring 1993), 90–107.

Monod, Paul Kléber, *Jacobitism and the English People, 1688–1788*, Cambridge: Cambridge University Press, 1989.
  The Power of Kings: Monarchy and Religion in Europe, 1589–1715, New Haven: Yale University Press, 1999.

Morris, Desmond, *The Naked Ape*, London: Jonathan Cape, 1967.

Nairn, Tom, *The Break-Up of Britain: Crisis and Neo-Nationalism*, London: Verso, 1981.
  The Enchanted Glass: Britain and its Monarchy, London: Radius, 1988.
  After Britain: New Labour and the Return of Scotland, London: Granta, 2000.

National Council for Civil Liberties, *Stonehenge. A Report into the Civil Liberties Implications of the Events Relating to the Convoys of Summer 1985 and 1986*, London: National Council for Civil Liberties, 1986.

Nettl, J. P., 'The German Social Democratic Party 1890–1914 as a Political Model', *Past and Present* 30 (April 1965), 65–95.

Newsinger, John, 'The American Connection: George Orwell, "Literary Trotskyism" and the New York Intellectuals', *Labour History Review* 64, 1, Spring (1999), 23–43.

North, Douglass C., *Structure and Change in Economic History*, New York: W. W. Norton, 1981.

Oakeshott., Michael, *On Human Conduct*, Oxford: Clarendon Press, 1975.

O'Kane, Rosemary H. T., 'Against Legitimacy', *Political Studies* 41, 3 (September 1993), 471–87.

Olson, Mancur, 'The Logic of Collective Action in Soviet-type Societies', *Journal of Soviet Nationalities* 1, Summer (1990), 8–27.

O'Neil, Patrick H., 'Revolution from Within: Institutional Analysis, Transitions from Authoritarianism, and the Case of Hungary', *World Politics* 48, 4 (July 1996), 579–603.

Orwell, George, *The Collected Essays, Journalism and Letters of George Orwell*, ed. Sonia Orwell and Ian Angus, 4 vols., Harmondsworth: Penguin, 1970.

Pakulski, Jan, 'Legitimacy and Mass Compliance: Reflections on Max Weber and Soviet-Type Societies', *British Journal of Political Science*, 16, 1 (1986), 35–56.

'Ideology and Political Domination: A Critical Re-appraisal', *International Journal of Comparative Sociology* 28, 3–4 (1987), 129–57.

'Poland: Ideology, Legitimacy and Political Domination' in Nicholas Abercrombie, Stephen Hill, and Bryan S. Turner (eds.), *Dominant Ideologies*, London: Unwin Hyman, 1990.

'East European Revolutions and "Legitimacy Crisis"' in Janina Frentzel-Zagórska (ed.), *From a One-Party State to Democracy*, Amsterdam: Rodopi, 1993.

Peake, Mervyn, *Titus Groan*, London: Eyre and Spotiswood, 1946.

Gormenghast, London: Eyre and Spotiswood, 1950.

Peterson, M. J., *Recognition of Governments: Legal Doctrine and State Practice*, 1815–1995, Basingstoke: Macmillan, 1997.

Przeworski, Adam, *Capitalism and Social Democracy*, Cambridge: Cambridge University Press, 1985.

Democracy and the Market: Political and Economic Reforms in Eastern Europe and Latin America, Cambridge: Cambridge University Press, 1991.

Raeff, Marc, 'The Well-Ordered Police State and the Development of Modernity in Seventeenth- and Eighteenth-Century Europe: An Attempt at a Comparative Approach', *American Historical Review* 80, 5 (1975), 1221–43.

Ranger, Terence and Vaughan, Olufemi (eds.), *Legitimacy and the State in Twentieth-Century Africa: Essays in Honour of A. H. M. Kirk-Greene*, London: Macmillan, 1993.

Rayner, Jeremy, 'Philosophy into Dogma: The Revival of Cultural Conservatism', *British Journal of Political Science* 16, 4 (October 1986), 455–74.

Reif, Karlheinz, 'Cultural Convergence and Cultural Diversity as Factors in European Identity' in Soledad Garcia (ed.), *European Identity and the Search for Legitimacy*, London: Pinter, 1993.

Richter, Melvin, 'Towards a Concept of Political Illegitimacy: Bonapartist Dictatorship and Democratic Legitimacy', *Political Theory* 10, 2 (May 1982), 185–214.

Rigby, T. H., 'Introduction: Political Legitimacy, Weber and Communist Mono-organisational Systems' in T. H. Rigby and Ferenc Féher (eds.), *Political Legitimation in Communist States*, New York: St. Martin's Press, 1982.

'Dominant and Subsidiary Modes of Political Legitimation in the USSR: A Comment on Christel Lane's Article', *British Journal of Poltical Science* 14 (1984), 219–22.

Rigby, T. H. and Féher, Ferenc (eds.), *Political Legitimation in Communist States*, New York: St. Martin's Press, 1982.

Ringmar, Erik, 'The Relevance of International Law: a Hegelian Interpretation of a Peculiar Seventeenth-Century Preoccupation', *Review of International Studies* 21 (1995), 87–103.

Identity, Interest and Action: A Cultural Explanation of Sweden's Intervention in the Thirty Years War, Cambridge: Cambridge University Press, 1996.

Risen, Jim and Thomas, Judy, *Wrath of Angels: The American Abortion War*, New York: Basic Books, 1997.

Robinson, Neil, 'What was Soviet Ideology? A Comment on Joseph Schull and an Alternative', *Political Studies* 43, 2 (June 1995), 325–32.

Rorty, Richard, *Contingency, Irony and Solidarity*, Cambridge: Cambridge University Press, 1989.

Rosen, Michael, *On Voluntary Servitude: False Consciousness and the Theory of Ideology*, Cambridge, MA: Harvard University Press, 1996.

Rothschild, Joseph, 'Observations on Political Legitimacy in Contemporary Europe', *Political Science Quarterly* 92, 3, Fall (1977), 487–501.

Rustow, Dankwart A. (ed.), *Philosophers and Kings: Studies in Leadership*, New York: George Braziller, 1970.

Sandler, Lucy Freeman, 'The Wilton Diptych and Images of Devotion in Illuminated Manuscripts' in Gillian Gordon, Lisa Monnas, and Caroline Elam (eds.), *The Regal Image of Richard II and the Wilton Diptych*, London: Harvey Miller Publishers, 1998.

Saward, Michael, *Co-optive Politics and State Legitimacy*, Aldershot: Dartmouth, 1992.

'Legitimacy and the State in Europe: Theories, Crises and Complexity' in J. J. Hesse and T. Toonen (eds.), *The European Yearbook of Comparative*

Government and Public Administration, vol. I, Boulder, and Baden-Baden: Westview and Nomos Verlagsgesellschaft, 1995.

Schaar, J. H., *Legitimacy in the Modern State*, New Brunswick, NJ: Transaction Books, 1970.

Schlozman, Kay Lehman, Verba, Sidney, and Brady, Henry E., 'Participation's Not a Paradox: The View from American Activists', *British Journal of Political Science* 25, 1 (January 1995), 1–36.

Schull, Joseph, 'What is Ideology? Theoretical Problems and Lessons from Soviet-Type Societies', *Political Studies* 40, 4, December (1992), 728–41.

Schumpeter, Joseph A., *Capitalism, Socialism, and Democracy*, 1943, 5th edn, London: George Allen and Unwin, 1976.

Scruton, Roger, *The Meaning of Conservatism*, Harmondsworth: Penguin, 1980, 2nd edn, 1984.

Selznick, Philip, 'Cooptation: A Mechanism for Organizational Stability' in R. K. Merton (ed.), *Reader in Bureaucracy*, Glencoe, IL: Free Press of Glencoe, 1964.

Shapin, Steven, *The Scientific Revolution*, Chicago: Chicago University Press, 1996.

Shaw, George Bernard, *Ruskin's Politics*, London: Ruskin Centenary Council, 1921.

Shils, E. and Young, M., 'The Sociological Meaning of the Coronation', *Sociological Review*, new series, 1 (1953), 63–81.

Smith, Anthony D., *National Identity*, Harmondsworth: Penguin, 1991.

Spencer, M. E., 'Weber on Legitimate Norms and Authority', *British Journal of Sociology* 21 (1970), 123–34.

Sperling, Susan, *Animal Liberators: Research and Morality*, London: University of California Press, 1988.

Sternberg, Dolf, 'Typologie de la légitimité' in P. Bastid *et al.*, *L'Idée de légitimité*, Paris: Presses Universitaires de France, 1967.

'Legitimacy' in David L. Sills (ed.), *The International Encyclopedia of the Social Sciences*, vol. IX, New York: Free Press, 1968.

Stillman, Peter G., 'The Concept of Legitimacy', *Polity* (Amherst: North Eastern Political Science Association), 7, 1 (Fall 1974), 32–56.

Stinchcombe, Arthur L., *Constructing Social Theories*, New York: Harcourt Brace, 1968.

Strohm, Paul, *England's Empty Throne: Usurpation and the Language of Legitimation, 1399–1422*, London: Yale University Press, 1998.

Sukatipan, Saitip, 'Thailand: The Evolution of Legitimacy' in Muthiah Alagappa, *Political Legitimacy in Southeast Asia: The Quest for Moral Authority*, Stanford: Stanford University Press, 1995.

Taylor, Charles, *Multiculturalism: Examining The Politics of Recognition*, ed. Amy Gutmann, 2nd edn, Princeton: Princeton University Press, 1994.

Teiwes, Frederick C., *Leadership, Legitimacy, and Conflict in China: From a Charismatic Mao to the Politics of Succession*, London: Macmillan, 1984.

Tester, Keith and Walls, John, 'The Ideology and Current Activities of the Animal Liberation Front', *Contemporary Politics* 2, 2, Summer (1996), 79–91.

Thompson, E. P., *Whigs and Hunters*, London: Allen Lane, 1975.

Toolis, Kevin, *Rebel Heart*, London: Picador, 1995.

Turner, Bryan S., 'Nietzsche, Weber, and the Devaluation of Politics: The Problem of State Legitimacy', *Sociological Review* 30 (1982), 367–91.

Tyler, Tom R., 'Justice, Self-interest, and the Legitimacy of Legal and Political Authority' in Jane J. Mansbridge, *Beyond Self-Interest*, Chicago: University of Chicago Press, 1990.

Vale, Lawrence J., *Architecture, Power and National Identity*, New Haven: Yale University Press, 1992.

Vernon, James (ed.), *Re-reading the Constitution: New Narratives in the Political History of England's Long Nineteenth Century*, Cambridge: Cambridge University Press, 1996.

Veyne, Paul, *Bread and Circuses: Historical Sociology and Political Pluralism*, trans. Brian Pearce, Harmondsworth: Penguin, 1992.

Vidich, Arthur J., 'Legitimation of Regimes in World Perspective' in Arthur J. Vidich and Ronald M. Glassman (eds.), *Conflict and Control: Challenges to Legitimacy of Modern Governments*, London: Sage, 1979.

Vidich, Arthur J. and Glassman, Ronald M. (eds.), *Conflict and Control: Challenges to Legitimacy of Modern Governments*, London: Sage, 1979.

Vrcan, Srdjan, 'A Different Historical Perspective on Legitimation', *Current Sociology* 35, 2 (1987), 127–34.

Walker, Rachel, 'Thinking about Ideology and Method: A Comment on Schull', *Political Studies* 43, 4 (June 1995), 333–42.

Wallace, Helen, 'Deepening and Widening: Problems of Legitimacy for the EC' in Soledad Garcia (ed.), *European Identity and the Search for Legitimacy*, London: Pinter, 1993.

Weale, Albert and Nentwich, Michael (eds.), *Political Theory and the European Union: Legitimacy, Constitutional Choice and Citizenship*, London: Routledge/ECPR, 1998.

Weatherford, M. Stephen, 'Measuring Political Legitimacy', *American Political Science Review* 86 (1992), 149–66.

Weber, Max, *Economy and Society*, ed. Guenther Roth and Claus Wittich, 2 vols., London: University of California Press, 1978.

Weil, Frederick D., 'The Sources and Structure of Legitimation in Western Democracies. A Consolidated Model Tested with Time-Series Data in Six Countries Since World War II', *American Sociological Review* 54 (1989), 682–706.

Weiler, J. H. H., 'After Maastricht: Community Legitimacy in Post-1992 Europe' in Adams (ed.), *Singular Europe: Economy and Polity of the European Community after 1992*, Ann Arbor: University of Michigan Press, 1992.

Wilentz, Sean (ed.), *Rites of Power: Symbolism, Ritual and Politics Since the Middle Ages*, Philadelphia: University of Pennsylvania Press, 1985.

'Introduction: Teufelsdröckh's Dilemma: On Symbolism, Politics, and History' in Sean Wilentz (ed.), *Rites of Power: Symbolism, Ritual and Politics Since the Middle Ages*, Philadelphia: University of Pennsylvania Press, 1985.

Williams, Howard, 'International Relations and the Reconstruction of Political Theory', *Politics* 14 (1994), 135–42.

Williams, John, *Legitimacy in International Relations and the Rise and Fall of Yugoslavia*, London: Macmillan, 1998.

Wills, Gary, 'The New Revolutionaries', *New York Review of Books* 42, 13, 10 August 1995, 50–5.

Wilson, Bryan, 'Religion and the Secular State' in S. J. D. Green and R. C. Whiting (eds.), *The Boundaries of the State in Modern Britain*, Cambridge: Cambridge University Press, 1996.

Wolin, S. S., 'Max Weber: Legitimation, Methods, and the Politics of Theory', *Political Theory* 9 (1981), 401–24.

Woodward, Jennifer, *The Theatre of Death: The Ritual Management of Royal Funerals in Renaissance England, 1570–1625*, Woodbridge: The Boydell Press, 1997.

Woolf, Virginia, *Three Guineas*, London: Hogarth Press, 1938, repr. London, Penguin, 1993.

Yawnghwe, C. T., 'Mystification and Rationality: Legitimacy and the State in the Third World', *Journal of Contemporary Asia* 22, 2 (1992), 169–86

Young, Hugo, *One of Us: A Biography of Margaret Thatcher*, London: Macmillan, 1989.

Zhong, Y., 'Legitimacy Crisis and Legitimation in China', *Journal of Contemporary Asia* 26, 2 (1996), 201–20.

Index

abortion, 102–3
Ahmad, Aijiz, 62
Akuapem, kings of, 53
Algeria, 125
Anderson, Benedict, 56
Anglo, Sydney, 55
Animal Liberation Front, 103
animal rights, 103
Appiah, K. Anthony, 128–9
architecture, 58
Ascherson, Neal, 95
Austin, Regina, 9 n.13
Australia, 127–8

Bagehot, Walter, 52
Bali, 55
banners, 116
Baylis, Thomas S., 78 n.21
Bebel, August, 100
Beer, S. H., 131
Beetham, David, 14–15, 22 n. 52, 24, 67, 86
Bensman, Joseph, 14, 37–8
Berger, Joseph, 46
Berger, Peter, 37, 44
Binski, Paul, 48, 54, 61
Black, David, 87
Blau, Peter, 33
Bourdieu, Pierre, 38, 57
Bourricaud, François, 23, 25
Brasília, 58
Bray, Michael, 102
Brazier, Margaret, 74 n.10
Bromley, 124
Burke, Edmund, 140
Burke, Peter, 52, 57, 83
Burma, 25

Cambodia, 25
Campbell, David, 22 n.51
Cannadine, David, 54 n.50, 58, 68, 77
Chan, Hok-lam, 93
Chandigarh, 58
Charles I, 97
Chesterton, G. K., 95
China, 56, 60
Christian right, USA, 102–3
Christianity, 102–3
citizens, 111–15
citizenship, European, 123
civil disobedience, 101–2
class, 7, 12, 73
Claude, Inis, 17, 50, 88
Cloth of Gold, Field of, 84
coercion, 101–2
cold war, 6, 12
communism, 78, 122
    collapse of in Eastern Europe and Soviet Union, 6, 7, 8, 14, 27, 65–7, 91
    communist rulers, 84
Connor, Walker, 121
co-option, 71–5
coronation, 5, 53
Czech Republic, 130

David, Louis, 5
democracy, 7, 124–8, 132–5
democratic legitimation, 111–12, 126
Deutsch, Karl, 37
di Palma, Guiseppi, 59–60, 67
diplomatic rituals, 83
divine right, 18, 91
Downs, Anthony, 2–3, 108
Dunleavy, Patrick, 74, 108

Eastern Europe,
  collapse of communism in, 6, 7, 8, 14,
    27, 65–7, 91
Easton, David, 16–17
Edelman, Murray, 49, 58
Egypt, 85
Eisenhower, President, 84
elections, 112–15
Elias, Norbert, 57–8, 75
elite theory, 108
elites, 71–5, 76–82, 96
enemies, 36, 128–32
Erikson, Erik, 49
European Court of Human Rights, 122
European Court of Justice, 122
European Union, 14–5, 27, 34, 64–5, 86,
    95, 122–3

Ferrell, Lori, 56, 86
Field of the Cloth of Gold, 84
Forbidden City, China, 48–9
Fox, Merritt, 48–9
Francis I, 84
Franck, Thomas, 84, 87
Friedrich, Carl, 16
Fulbrook, Mary, 78
funerals, 56–7, 76

Geertz, Clifford, 6, 55, 99
Germany, 63, 78
Glassman, Ronald, 20–1
Goffman, Erving, 31
Goodin, Robert, 44
Goodsell, Charles, 82–3
Gramsci, Antonio, 79, 100
Green, Donald, 113, 114
Green, S. J. D., 134
Greenfeld, Liah, 131, 133
Griffin, Michael, 102
Gurr, Ted, 104
Gypsies, 130

Halliwell, David, 98
Hardin, Russell, 61–2
Harington, Sir John, 97
Heisler, M. O., 71–2
Henry III, 15, 47–8
Henry V, 48
Henry VII, 55
Henry VIII, 84
Henshaw, David, 103 n.45

Hinze, Otto, 37
Hirschman, Albert O., 40
Hitler, Adolf, 82–3, 109
Hobsbawm, Eric, 7, 62, 79, 98
Holmes, Leslie, 66
Hooghe, Liesbet, 64 n.80
Hroch, Miroslav, 62, 96
Hungary, 91
Hurd, Douglas, 130
Huskey, Eugene, 21
Hussein, Sadam, 48

identification and legitimation, 31–5,
    119–21
identity/identification, 35–6
imams, 82
inaugural lectures, 1
IRA, 92, 97–8, 105
Iraq, 48
Islam, 81–2, 93, 125

Jacobites, 98–9
James I & VI, 56, 87
Java, 56
Josephine, Empress, 5

Kantorowicz, Ernst, 54 n.48, 49
Kedward, H. R., 90
Kepel, Gilles, 82
Kertzer, David, 99
Kipling, Rudyard, 11
Klotz, Audie, 87
Kremlin, 48–9
Khrushchev, Nikita, 84
Kubik, Jan, 66
Kvavik, Robert, 71–2

language, 56
Laski, Harold, 32
Lasswell, Harold, 48–9
Lawrence, Jon, 79
Lazzaretti, Davide, 97
Lee, Ronnie, 103 n.44
Leeson, R. A., 115 n.21
legitimacy
  distinguished from legitimation, 2,
    17–18, 22–4
  empirically or historically assessed, 8,
    9–10
  fusion of normative and empirical
    theories, 11–12
  normatively assessed, 4–5, 8–9, 11, 21–3

Index

legitimation
  and compliance, 117–19
  and co-option, 71–5
  and democracy, 109ff.
  and ethical coherence, 36–8
  and privacy, 54–8, 68–9
  and public support, 42–4, 107–9
  and types of rule, 38–9, 64–5
  crises, 24
  distinguished from legitimacy, 2, 17–18,
    22–4
  endogenous/self-legitimation, 3–6,
    28–9, 30–1, 45–54
  failures of, 65–8, 121–4
  new attention paid to, 12–15
  of citizens, 111–15
  of leaders and of followers, 58–61, 75–8
  of rulers by rulers, 70–1, 82–8
  possible objections to theory of, 16–17
  three groups of actors, 42, 70–1
Levi, Margaret, 73, 118–19
Lewis, Paul G., 65
liberalism, economic, 7
Liberty Tree, 99
Lijphart, Arendt, 132–3
Linz, Juan, 33
Lipset, S. M., 126
Little Malcolm, 98
liturgy, 44
local government, 124
Lord, Christopher, 14–15, 22 n.52, 24, 67,
  86
Louis XIV, 52, 53, 57–8, 77, 83
Lovecy, Jill, 74 n.10
Luckman, Thomas, 37

Machiavelli, Niccolò, 3, 47
Mackenzie, W. J. M., 62
Mandarin language, 56
maquis, 90
Marr, Andrew, 105
Marxism, 7, 57, 65, 84
mass, 44
Maurras, Charles, 90
McAllister, Ian, 127–8
McCauley, Martin, 65
McLean, Iain, 113
Mill, John Stuart, 47
Mitterand, François, 52
modernity, 6
monarchy, 15, 53, 56–8, 60–1, 63–4, 70
Moran, Michael, 74 n.10

Morris, Desmond, 140
Morris, William, 136

Nairn, Tom, 95
Napoleon, 5
nationalism, 7, 61–4, 79–82, 94–6
Nazism, 63, 82–3, 99
Nettl, J. P., 100
new age travellers, 129–30
North, Douglass C., 73, 118–19
Northern Ireland, 91–2

O'Neil, Patrick, 91
Oakeshott, Michael, 132
Olson, Mancur, 21, 67
Operation Rescue, 102
Ordeshook, Peter, 113
Orwell, George, 92, 95
Ottoman empire, 85

Paine, Tom, 140
Pakistan, 97
Pakulski, Jan, 14, 65–6, 121
papacy, 122
Pareto, Vilfredo, 94
Paris Commune, 99–100
Parson, Talcott, 126
patriarchy, 81
Pol Pot, 25
Poland, 14, 66, 84, 115, 121
poll tax, 124
post-modernity, 6, 12
Potton, Margaret, 74 n.10
power, 2–3
prestige, 2–5
priesthood, 44
prisoner's dilemma, 118
Przeworkski, Adam, 100
Pye, Lucien, 62

Qutb, Sayyid, 93

Raeff, Marc, 73
Ranger, Terence, 55
rational choice theory, 112–13
rebellion, 89–94
rebels, 89–94, 97–101
Reifenstahl, Leni, 63
religion, 7, 81–2, 93, 102–3, 125
Renner, Karl, 79
Richard III, 54
Richter, Melvin, 20

Rigby, T. H., 60
Riker, William, 113
Ringmar, Erik, 85 n.48
Roma, 130
Roman Catholic Church, 122
Rorty, Richard, 18–19, 131
Rosen, Michael, 100–1, 117–18,
    121, 137
Rothschild, Joseph, 14, 65
Rushdie, Salman, 82
Russian Revolution 1917, 7

Saltaire, 75
Saward, Michael, 73
Schull, Joseph, 57
Schumpeter, Joseph A., 108
science, 32
scientists, 32
Scotland, 95, 124
Scruton, Roger, 119
sects, religious, 122
Selznick, Philip, 72
Serbia, 87
sermons, 56, 87
Shapiro, Ian, 113, 114
shari'a, 93
Sharif, Nawaz, 97
Shaw, George Bernard, 108
SLORC, 25
Smith, Anthony D., 133
Social Democratic Party (SPD), Germany,
    100
South Africa, 87
Southwark, 124
Soviet Union, 57, 83
    collapse of communism in, 6, 7, 8
Stammler, Rudolph, 18
state, 2, 134
Sternberg, Dolf, 46–7, 91
Stillman, Peter, 20
Strohm, Paul, 48
Stuarts, 98–0
Sukatipan, Saitip, 6 n.6
Sweden, 85

Taylor, Charles, 119 n.30
Teiwes, Frederick, 60
Terry, Randall, 102
Thailand, 6 n.6
Thatcher, Margaret, 120, 130
theocracy, 92–3, 104

Thorne, Will, 81
Tocqueville, Alexis de, 20
Toolis, Kevin, 97 n.20–1, 98 n.22
Tower Hamlets, 124
trade unions, 116
Turner, Bryan, 31
twentieth century, short, 6, 7

United Kingdom, 95–6, 134
United Nations, 84

Vaughan, Olufemi, 55
Vernon, James, 115 n.20
Versailles, 75, 83
Veyne, Paul, 47, 52–3
Vichy regime, 90
Victoria, Queen, 76–7
Vidich, Arthur, 20–1, 86
vigilantes, 101–3
voting, 112–15

Wales, 95, 124
Wallace, Helen, 86
Weatherman, 101
Weber, Max 18, 19–20, 31, 33
    account of legitimation, 2, 4, 17–18,
        19–20
    confusions by and misunderstandings of,
        17–19
    criticisms of, 19–21
    elective affinity, 50
    on democracy, 111, 126
    on justification of action, 37–8, 45–6,
        113, 118
    on leaders and followers, 58–9
    on relation between type of legitimation
        and type of regime, 38–9, 64–5
    on self-legitimation, 4, 5, 12–14, 45
Weimar Republic, 78
Westminster Abbey, 15, 54, 61
White House, 49
Whiting, R. C., 134
William IV, 76–7
Wilton Diptych, 54
Wood, Stewart, 113
Woodward, Jennifer, 56–7
Woolf, Virginia, 140

Xedong, Mao, 60

Zelditch, Morris, 46